Praise for Joseph Rosendo's *Musings*

Musings is a must read, a worldwide journey to the far reaches of the planet, each page richly energetic and full of magic. With enormous observational skills and humor, Joseph Rosendo has shared a Cuban American life and a lifetime of memories. Rosendo is in his own special space and is the travel voice of our time.

Richard Carroll
Award-Winning Travel Journalist

Joseph Rosendo has the curiosity of a scholar, uses language like a poet, and has assembled a lovely mosaic of a book drawn from his decades of global travels and musings. He has a novelist's eye for the telling details, and a reporter's knack for the revealing quote. In Musings, there is no hiding under the desk. These collected essays are like Chopin's nocturnes: timeless, transcendent, universal. One does not so much read them as fall under their spell.

Richard Bangs
Adventures with Purpose

In Musings, Joseph Rosendo expresses the kind of warmth and humanity that have made Travelscope so successful. Reading this mix of practical advice and evocative storytelling is like having the popular television host take you on a personal tour of some of his favorite places and listening as he entertains you with touching and funny experiences. His sense of humor and his passion for travel make this book a joy to read.

Elizabeth Harryman, *SATW* President and Paul Lasley
Cohosts, *OnTravel*, American Forces Network

I have known Joseph Rosendo for nearly twenty years and it has been my distinct pleasure to have been involved in the sponsoring of Travelscope both on radio and on television. To understand Joseph's passion for travel and "what makes him tick?" you need only to read this book. More than an autobiography, Musings is filled with the kind of insight, humor, travel tips and opinions that serve to shine a spotlight on Joseph Rosendo, the man. When you finish Musings you will fully understand why Joseph's travel endeavors have been and continue to be so successful. Whether you're a novice or experienced traveler, "Musings" should be required reading.

Geoff Colquitt, former Marketing Director
DK Eyewitness Travel

The man behind the travel television show reveals himself through wisdom, humor, curiosity and — always — passion. Musings is not a guide for sightseeing. It is a life story that reveals, from start to finish, the soul of Joseph and what makes him fully engaged in the world. I recommend it as inspiration before your next travels.

Candace De Puy, Ph.D.
Author of *The Healing Choice*

Musings gives us an image of how beautiful and important to our consciousness travel is. Joseph's travel and personal stories reveal the foundation of his respect for international community that is portrayed in his PBS television show, Joseph Rosendo's Travelscope.

Deni Leonard
Native American Elder

Musings

The Short Happy Pursuit
of Pleasure and Other Journeys

Joseph Rosendo

Dedication

Above all, this book is dedicated to my wife, Julie,
without whom there would not be all of
what is wonderful in my life.

It is also dedicated to my abuelita Maria
and my "Tia" Blanca,
who taught me about unconditional love,
and to my grandchildren Loretta, Wally, Zoe and Josiah,
who infuse my life with joy and let me stay childlike.

And, finally, to my brother Ron.
"He was my friend, my fan and my witness."
I miss you every day.

Table of Contents

Introduction

For me the art of writing grew out of the art of talking. I spoke, therefore I wrote. Writing did have a monastic quality to it for me because although some people are driven to write, I, on the other hand, have to be driven to a monk's cell, whipped into submission and forced to write — and after forty years of being a travel writer I'd say that's a pretty good description of what a deadline does.

Merriam-Webster's New Collegiate Dictionary's definition of the noun Musing is "Meditation." The adjective's definition is "thoughtfully abstracted: meditative." When I first started writing my Musings column it was at the urging of Ann McCarthy, my new Travelscope publication editor, and I never dreamt I was meditating.

I had always spouted off about the Art of Travel and since becoming the host of the PBS television series *Joseph Rosendo's Travelscope*, I've spoken of Travel As A Life-Changing Experience at travel shows, wellness expos, embassies, schools, coffee shops, bus stops and street corners around the world. I speak to whomever will listen and some that would rather not. People close to me and at distant tables often hear me ranting and raving about how travel can bring people together and change the world. It may be a Travel-And-Save-The-World '60s view of the experience, but then, I am particularly fond of those good-old hippie days. Anyway, back in the mists of time Ann, the new editor of the travel newsletter I was doing in the 1980s, which became an online magazine in the 2000s, suggested that among many changes there should be a column where I could safely (and quietly) ramble on about whatever I

wanted. And since my ramblings often connected formerly unrelated events, topics, concepts and ideas — "Musings" seemed like a good name for them.

The funny thing is now that I've rediscovered the dictionary definition I realize that writing Musings back then *was* a meditative process. It was a time when I was forced to allow my mind to wander through the back alleys of my life propelled by the unifying thread of travel.

Many of the musings, particularly the earlier ones,

were directly related to travel. They were destination pieces and how-to offerings on bargaining, packing, planning and other nuts-and-bolts travel issues. Soon others sprouted up that were less solidly connected to travel as an activity, and finally, the thread seemed to snap altogether. I wrote about my childhood travels, my year of spring, my Cuban grandparents, my quest for the holy platter, my brunch-conquering brother and other happenings. My musings began to describe my own personal journey.

Strangely enough writing about the stops along my own sojourn didn't seem much different than writing a travel story. The final destination was always clear, but what would happen along the way was not. Both adventures included brief stops where I picked up things that I could use later on the trip. Some of these things proved a burden and had to be dumped, but most of them came in handy. I discovered that if you were to happily survive both — travel and life — you should keep your sense of humor and be as adaptable as possible. And that you should never, never ever, isolate yourself from the experience and just observe from a place apart — sightseeing, if you will. Instead you must commit yourself to what's happening and relish the good, the bad and the ugly of it. "May you live all the days of your life," said Jonathan Swift. "And may you savor the journey along the way," I'd add.

So, over the years these musings were written. They span across thirty years. There are references that are dated (my iPhone has replaced my tape recorder, for instance, and I don't carry film anymore), but like travel memories, at their heart and in spirit they are evergreen. Lately they've been tweaked, polished and augmented a bit and I've added an introduction to each. They touch on many topics, but the voyage, the passage, is always the subtext.

I've been told that writers should never apologize for their work or draw readers' attention to any faults. While I expect I owe you a few of the former and you will discover several of the latter without my help, I will say this: These musings were written over a long period of time and designed to stand alone with no reference to each other. Now that they're together you might notice several have similar themes. I left them all in because either I felt that the presentations were different enough to offer a valuable perspective on a topic or I just liked something about them too much to not include them. If they seem repetitious and bore you then I'll simply ask your forgiveness and suggest you skip on to the next one.

In creating this book I had the opportunity to become reacquainted with my family in an intimate way. When I cropped, adjusted and beautified the family pictures, I was able to meet them again — up close and personal.

I was reminded how fastidious my brother was about his attire; how he loved his coat and tie and would dress up for any occasion. The stacks of photos I went through rekindled my memories of the hilarious and harrowing adventures we shared and the obstacles we overcame.

I particularly enjoyed working on my grand-mother Maria's portrait as a 17-year-old newlywed. I never knew her as a young woman, just as my *Wita*, my childhood pronunciation of *abuelita*, "grandmother" in Spanish. I realized what a great beauty she was and it was a thrill to discover when I zoomed in that the pin she's wearing on her collar contains my grandfather's image.

Except for *The Fear of Travel* sketches by Sharon Berryhill, all illustrations for my musings are by artist Barbara Taylor and taken from the original Travelscope Newsletters. Barbara would draw them to fit space and story and then "old school style," paste up each issue. She also designed the publication and created the Travelscope logo, which we still use. I'm beholden to her for lending her talents to my endeavors.

I want to thank Ann McCarthy, Ph.D., who came out of copyeditor retirement "this one time" to proof the book. She and Frank Walsh, her husband and my oldest and dearest friend, were my go-to counselors on whether something worked or not.

Friends, family or myself took most of the pictures in *Musings*, but I especially want to credit Julie Rosendo, Travis Feuerbacher, Gili Dekel, and Bruce Royer for their photographic contributions. And a special thanks goes out to photographer Frank Walsh for lending his eye and expertise to improving my amateur Photoshop efforts.

I'm eternally grateful to my wife, Julie, who I've worked with arm-in-arm on *Joseph Rosendo's Travelscope* for more than a decade. Well aware of the inherent risks in critiquing my work, she read my writings and still gave me her honest opinion.

Finally, I'm forever indebted to the people I've met around the world who inspired *Musings*. And to those friends, readers, writers and editors who encouraged me to write them and finally publish them, I offer my heartfelt gratitude.

On the book's back cover I express the hope that my tales will be a journey of discovery. Certainly choosing the stories, composing the introductions and selecting the images was a rite of passage for me. In the process of resurrecting ancient writings, illustrations and photos, I wandered through past days, events and relationships and dug up manifestations of myself that I hadn't encountered recently. The experience was humbling and illuminating, as well as reaffirming and reassuring.

If my meditations anger, amuse or touch you, I'm happy. If they don't, I understand. I'm just pleased you came along for the ride.

Happy Traveling!

Topanga, California
Summer 2020

The Art of Travel

I'd Leave — If I Could Pack My Bags

I published my first travel story in the Los Angeles Times in 1980, started a travel radio show on KIEV in Los Angeles in 1985 and Joseph Rosendo's Travelscope first aired on PBS station KLRN in San Antonio, Texas in 2005. In my younger travel writer days I traveled weighed down by a huge backpack stuffed with a large Sony cassette tape recorder, two Canon cameras, several lens, writing materials and all the accessories. That's when I learned the true value of a good Thai back mass-age. My wife Julie will report that after all those decades of traveling I have still not learned how to pack for myself. Some people are dyslexic, I'm packing challenged, which is what inspired me to write the following early Musing.

On location in Greenville, Tennessee
(1996)

9

I hate to pack. And even though I've been a travel journalist for many, many years, I still haven't figured out how to do it easily. I mean it's just one decision after another.

I tried each and every packing tip. I've made lists, and ended up spending more time making the list than packing. I got stumped on accessories. How do you accessorize a white shirt and black suit? Wear brown socks?

I've tried putting everything I want to take on the bed and putting half back. I can never decide on which half to put back. I thought about hiring someone to pack for me, but I couldn't afford it — I wouldn't trust them anyway.

Yet, every suitcase has a velvet lining, and after much trial and mostly error, I finally came up with a  solution that works — a travel uniform. Every travel uniform is made to satisfy basic needs. I start with a Gore-Tex outer coat with lots of pockets for stuffing my tape recorder, film, notepad and pens. My jacket has so many pockets, I sometimes misplace things.

Underneath my jacket I wear a raw silk safari-style shirt that I had made in Mumbai, India. I don't know if Mumbai's tailors are noted for making fashionable clothes, but they're fast. It was finished in a day and since I never have clothes made at home, it was fun. Isn't that one of the reasons we travel?

10

My pants are heavy cotton. Cotton because it's cool and heavy because, as my mother used to say, I'm "rough on clothes." And I've gotten considerably rougher over the years.

A pair of comfortable shoes is essential to a travel uniform. I have a pair that is all-purpose — good looks and comfortable.

Depending on the destination I may take a hat. I have one I bought for Nepal that is rain resistant and has wool flaps that can be brought down over the ears

Battling the winds at Ireland's Cliffs of Moher (1998)

and attach under the chin. Not stylish, but great in high winds — besides, it makes me feel like an adventurer.

I have incorporated into my travel uniform my favorite bit of clothing: "my travel writer's tee-shirt."

I picked it up at Banana Republic years ago. It has a map of Tanzania on the front, but the reason I wear it is the quote on the back.

It's by Mark Twain and reads, "Travel is fatal to prejudice, bigotry and narrow-mindedness." It reminds me why I pack my "travel uniform" and seek out the travel experience.

Cracking the Group Tour Nut

I've never been a big fan of group tours, especially the stereotypical "If it's Tuesday, it must be Belgium" variety. I'm glad to report that recently tour companies have heard their clients' grumblings and have developed programs that allow travelers time to roam on their own and have a more authentic travel experience. My first group trip was in 1969 when I was part of a USO tour out of UCLA performing

The UCLA USO tour, newly arrived in Kaiserslautern,
West Germany (1969)

"How to Succeed in Business Without Really Trying" for the U.S. troops stationed in Germany, most of them on the way to Vietnam. It was a life-changing experience in many ways. For one, it's when I became hooked on the dream of traveling around the world discovering, learning and growing for the rest of my life. Within ten years I would embark on my 40-year career and life as a travel journalist.

I just returned from a press trip to Portugal. A press trip is not unlike any other special interest escorted tour. We were a group of journalists in search of the essence of Portugal. Failing that, we would settle for finding something new and different to interest our audiences and readers.

We could just as well have been a group of history teachers paying homage to Portugal's ancient mariners, or wine lovers looking for the perfect glass of *porto tinto*. And just like those original European tourists, Hannibal and his elephants, we came, we saw, we conquered — and we did it as a group.

There is a lot to be said for escorted group tours. There's the warm camaraderie of your fellows, the expertise of the guides and the easy style of travel. There's always someone there to answer your questions, heft your bags, get you up and tell you where to go. If you have any problems there's help, and in foreign countries there's an interpreter.

What most escorted group tours lack is adventure. Everything is planned, scheduled and predictable. The reason most of us travel in the first place is to break the pattern of our everyday lives. We certainly don't want to exchange one dull routine for another. But it is possible to have your tour and some adventure, too.

Here are a few suggestions:

1. Make sure that your tour includes free time — golden time, I call it — unstructured time to explore on your own.
2. Don't choose an itinerary so packed that you'll be too exhausted to take advantage of the free time.
3. Buy a good guidebook or download it from the Internet. It introduces you to the country and maximizes your free time by nudging you in the right direction.
4. Ask for help from a local. A smile and a good phrasebook will usually overcome the language barrier, and who knows? It could be the beginning of a beautiful relationship.
5. Take a chance. Don't be foolish, but be brave.

After five days of being led around by our expert guides in Portugal, I got lazy. When we were set free to roam on our own, I felt disoriented. I thought I had lost the travel knack, but after a few friendly encounters with the locals, it came back.

Jack London once said about writing, "Don't loaf and invite inspiration; light out after it with a club, and if you don't get it you will nonetheless get something that looks remarkably like it."

A travel experience is like that. You can't just

wait for interesting things to materialize or be created for you. It's your trip — go out and make something happen! You're likely to end up with what you hope for or something better.

Home for the Holidays

In my Cuban family Christmas was the highlight of the year. Noche Buena, Christmas Eve, was celebrated at my abuelo and abuelita's boarding house on N.W. Ninth Street and Miami Avenue with much food, drink, music, dancing and Cuban cigars. Moving to California in 1968 to attend UCLA made going Home for the Holidays an adventure. Two years after I arrived, my brother Ron left Miami and joined me in Los Angeles so our journey home for Christmas became a joint venture. We traveled for three days across the country (stopping a night in New Orleans was a must) using a Driveaway scheme where we drove a car between Los Angeles and Miami in exchange for a free tank of gas and the "free" transportation. All the family holiday drama we encountered once we got home often made us wonder why we went through all the trouble.

It's holiday travel time, a time of year when we're all busy as elves making plans to go "home for the holidays."

Home for the holidays ... sounds cozy, doesn't it? We all have sugarplum visions of warm family reunions. It's a powerful lure, pulling at us from across the miles. The trick is to take the bait without getting hooked.

But I understand. I'm a sucker for home and holidays, as well. I was raised in Miami, Florida and each winter the moment the thermometer dropped to 75 degrees and the humidity sank to 95% — I could just feel Christmas in the air.

To me Christmas is tinsel and bubble lights, the smell of good things to eat and the one time you could count on adults to be filled with good cheer. It's a time filled with hopes and wishes and expectations — some satisfied and many not.

For years I went home to Miami every Christmas in search of pieces of that vision. Now I stay put or go elsewhere. But for those of you heading home, here are eight survival tips. There's room for you to add your own as you go.

GETTING THERE:

PLAN WAY AHEAD — If you're reading this and you haven't made plans already, you can ignore the next five suggestions.

DON'T FLY STANDBY — Winter weather is unpredictable and holiday flights are packed.

You don't want to spend Christmas circling Denver or Chicago or New York ... (You get the picture).

BE PATIENT & KIND — Remember everyone is as stressed out as you are. Try spreading a little holiday spirit around.

ONCE THERE:

STAY ELSEWHERE — Consider spending part of your stay in a motel, hotel, inn, resort, whatever nearby. It's the best way to not wear out your welcome. You may save a little cash staying under the family roof, but you'll pay for it later.

HAVE YOUR OWN WHEELS — If things get tough, you can make a quick getaway.

YOU CAN'T GO HOME AGAIN — Thomas Wolfe was right! Lower your expectations. Everyone becomes undependable at holiday time. It's not their fault — 'tis the season.

BETTER IDEAS?

GO ON VACATION — A true gift to yourself — and others. See your family at a time without Christmas tensions, like Labor Day.

STAY HOME — If it's a home for the holidays you want, how about yours?

And finally, remember that although many situations are as good as you make them, others come with built-in problems and are out of your control. At this time of year avoid dangers, play it safe and survive.

"And so, as Tiny Tim observed, 'God bless us Every One.'"

The Best Price

I learned the art of bargaining during the summers I spent with my dad selling avocados and mangos in the Black American neighborhoods of Miami, Florida. A depression era kid, unskilled and under-educated, my dad made money however he could. In addition to his regular 3am to 2pm stint as a White Belt Dairy milkman's assistant, where he shoveled ice and delivered milk, he spent every day hustling day jobs. Yet, although he worked several jobs each day, he never missed taking us kids to South Beach. On the way to the beach we'd stop in the nearby Black American neighborhood of Overtown, formerly called "Colored Town" and founded with Miami in 1896 as a place to isolate the Black men who worked on the railroad and helped build Miami. It was a close-knit, self-sustaining community of 50,000 citizens then and dubbed "The Harlem of the South." That was before it was cut into quarters by the I-95 and I-395 freeways in the 1960s and the population reduced to less than 9,000. The people were of African, Bahamian, Cuban and Haitian origins and they all knew and liked my dad greeting him as, "Jo Jo — The Mango Man." With my brother, Ron, and me looking on, they'd banter and haggle and my dad sold our fruit. Anxious to get us to the beach, my dad was always willing to agree on "the best price." I spent many childhood summers in Overtown and even before I knew Mark Twain's quote, "Travel is Fatal to Prejudice, Bigotry and Narrow-mindedness," I learned its meaning. Spending time in the presence of people who were segregated, oppressed, misused and abused by many taught me that no matter their race or creed, at heart, all people are the same and deserve to be treated with kindness and respect. I also picked up some awesome bargaining tips.

The Mango Man and his sons on South Beach (c. 1972)

"To bargain or not to bargain, that is the question.
Whether 'tis nobler in the mind to suffer
the slings and arrows of haggling
or to pay the asking price and end them."
with apologies to Shakespeare and Hamlet

Ah, there's the rub.

How many times have we purchased a local handicraft only to discover that our friend got the same item for half the price — because he bargained for it.

Ah, do not then "the slings and arrows of outrageous fortune" sting us? How to get the "best price" and when, where and how you should bargain is the subject of my next book, *Bargaining Your Vacation Away*. But until it reaches the publication stage, which I understand follows the writing stage; here are a few of my thoughts on the subject.

To begin with, my bargaining credo is, "If you choose to play the game — play it well and for all you're worth — within reason." The reasonable point being that the process remains friendly, fun and profitable for all concerned. (Yes, that especially includes the vendor.)

With Whom To Bargain

No sexism intended, but I prefer men. Perhaps, since they are more irresponsible and impractical than women, they enjoy the haggling game more and are more willing to compromise.

When To Bargain

1. First and Foremost, bargain only where it is culturally acceptable. Some bargaining meccas are:

Hong Kong, India, China, Mexico and most countries in Latin America. Not so much Europe — although the *brocantes* of France and *mercados de pulgas* of Spain, flea markets, are definitely a bargain hunter's paradise. In these places and countries and many others, you are expected to bargain. If you don't haggle, you will probably over-pay and lose face. Wheeling and Dealing is acceptable in open-air markets and stalls, but not usually in retail shops although it doesn't hurt to ask for a discount, especially if you are purchasing several items.

I just returned from Fiji and if you like to bargain, you'll love Sigatoka. The town is a "Let's Make A Deal" center. Prices on everything from shell jewelry and wooden cannibal forks (unused) to tee shirts and electronic equipment are negotiable. In the Central Market the bargaining frenzy is downright intense and not for the faint of heart.

In the Market, cut the asking price by 50% and hold your ground. Now, don't expect to get great quality at these bargain basement prices. In Fiji, as elsewhere, "you get what you pay for." Jack's of Fiji offers guarantees and higher prices. Baravi Handicrafts, located about 13 kilometers from Sigatoka towards Suva, was universally recommended as an honest shop with "quality goods and the best prices."

2. Bargain when you don't know the fair price of an item. By offering a lower price you'll soon get a good idea of the real value.

3. Bargain when the salesperson offers to you "the best price." You've been invited to haggle, so feel free to make an offer.

4. Ask for a discount when you've purchased a quantity of goods in one store.

When Not To Bargain

1. Don't bargain if you feel proposing less than is asked is taking unfair advantage of a person's economic situation. The Center for Responsible Tourism's *Traveler's Code of Ethics* offers this guideline: "When you are shopping remember that the bargain you obtained was possible only because of the low wages paid to the craftsman."

   In Fiji, at the pottery village of Nakabuta, seven kilometers from Sigatoka on the River Valley Road, I was invited into the village and shown how their native pottery was made. I met the women potters, talked with them and laughed with them. When they showed me their goods, I bought something. I did not bargain; it was not appropriate to do so. My purchase was more about thanking them for their hospitality than getting a deal.

2. Don't bargain whenever it makes you or your traveling companion uncomfortable. Remember the experience must be fun for all involved.

How To Bargain

1. Be prepared to walk away.
2. Be firm, but flexible.
3. Don't want the item too much or, at least, too obviously too much.
4. Have some idea of what the item would cost at home. This will allow you to know whether the "best price" is really a good value.
5. Don't let your well-intentioned friends make you feel cheap or guilty because you want to wheel and deal a bit. If you follow my guidelines, you'll have nothing to feel guilty about. You are doing what is expected and relating to the locals in a significant and personal way. Don't confuse charity with commerce.
6. Always bargain with good humor and a sense of fun. Find out about your vendor and share something about yourself with them. This is a human interaction with a craftsperson, artist or small business owner, not General Motors. I decide what an item is worth to me and that's what I offer — sometimes I get my price, most often I don't, but I am always rewarded with an excellent adventure.

Do It Now!

I produced and hosted a nationally syndicated travel radio show for twenty-three and half years and callers to the show often asked me when is the best time to travel. Perhaps because I was the Consulting Editor for DK Eyewitness Travel's "Where To Go When" and "Where To Go When – The Americas" I shouldn't be surprised. However, it's hard to answer that question when everyone has different reasons to travel, different times they can travel and unique interests. So, my answer is usually, it depends. It depends on the weather, cost, crowds, accessibility, etc. Yet, "it depends" doesn't always satisfy everyone. Unfortunately, since I don't pack a crystal ball in my luggage along with my toiletry kit, socks, shorts and running shoes, in the end, their guess is as good as mine.

The 1,092nd and last Travelscope Radio broadcast after more than 23 years on the air (December 20, 2008)

"So, when's the best time to go?" the caller demanded.

"What do you mean?" I replied.

"When is the weather good, the prices lowest and the things I want to see open? This trip's a big investment for me — time, money, energy. I want everything to be perfect."

"I've given you my suggestions," I said. "We can talk more about averages and maybes and most likelys, but there are no guarantees."

"I want everything to be perfect," he repeated.

"I know, but there are no guarantees ..." I paused. "Except one."

"One," he said, considering my offer.

"Well, one's something," he continued. "Because this time I'd like the trip to go the way it's supposed to. I know that in summer everything is open and the weather is good, but that's when the crowds come and things are more expensive. And, I have a friend who went there one summer and it rained the whole time. I want it the way it's supposed to be."

"I know," I said. "It's nice when that happens — when things are the way we want them to be. Still, the only thing I can tell you is that now is the best time to go and if you go now — well, you will have gone — that's my only guarantee."

"Huh?" he said, perturbed. "That's it? If I go now then I will have gone? That's pretty obvious."

"It is, isn't it?" I replied.

"Yeah, well, now is not the best time to go — I've

read that. So, thanks anyway. Thanks for your help."
And then he hung up.

Geez, I didn't even get to say I was sorry.

I hadn't been much help. I'd spent forty-five minutes on the phone giving advice, but I'd not given him what he wanted — a guarantee.

I wasn't trying to be a smart aleck. There are few guarantees to be had in the world. In fact, life only comes with one — that none of us will get out of here alive. And that's why I told him now was the best time to go.

It was good advice. I saw it on a poster in the '60s: "Live each day as if it was your last — because someday it will be." I didn't expect to pick up a philosophy of life from a poster, but this bit of pop philosophy has stuck with me as true.

Then there's the "Do not leave for tomorrow what you can do today" dictum. I never took it as the Calvinistic/Puritan work ethic admonition that it is, but as a warning — indeed, someday there won't be a tomorrow. And then there's always *carpe diem* — "Seize the day." It seems folks have been handing out this kind of advice for eons.

Now, I'm not trying to scare anyone. I don't think the End Days are here. People who predict The End Is Near are just wishful thinking. They're angry that their world will end someday and they want company. Louis XV felt like that — *"Après moi le déluge,"* he said. "After me the flood." Well, the flood never passed, but Louis did and the rest of us will.

My biggest fear is that I will have missed

something. I'm afraid that I won't get said all that needs to be said, see all I want to see, and do all I want to do. In fact, it's certain I won't get to everything — but, at least, I can die trying.

So, I gulp my wines, kiss my kitties, love my wife, relish sunsets, write my words — try to follow my own advice. And when I get sidetracked down trivial paths, when I get bogged down and hung up, when I let "things" steal my precious time, I try to remind myself that I don't have time to waste. I've got to do it — now.

Sounds like a sneaker ad, doesn't it? "Just Do It."

In spite of the forum, it's good advice. If you don't "Just Do It," it won't get done. And that would be a tragedy because if you don't do it or say it, it won't get said or done — not in your way. Instead, once you've acted, it's finished and nothing and nobody can ever take that away.

It's the only guarantee — do it and it will be done. "Do It Now" — before time runs out.

Location,
Location, Location

Alexandria Wager

As a travel journalist I've done my fair share of traveling en masse, but if you like traveling as a city rather than an individual nothing beats the mega cruise ship experience. Perhaps that's why in fifty years of traveling abroad, I've only done three of them. After going from the Egyptian Museum in Cairo to the Great Sphinx of Giza in seven buses and feeling like an invading expeditionary force, my inclination was to strike off on my own and cast my fate to the wind. Betting on the fact that alone was the best way to see Alexandria, our port-of-call, I discovered on a nighttime visit, that it is not without risks.

Cunard Cruise Lines' *MS Vistafiord* has docked in Alexandria, Egypt and it's my first chance to explore ashore on my own. With 700 of my fellow passengers I've spent the day on a shore excursion to Cairo to see the Pyramids, the Sphinx and the treasures of King Tutankhamun's tomb housed in the Egyptian Antiquities Museum.

There's a saying, "There are two types of people in the world — those who have seen the pyramids and those who have not." The same could be said for Alexandria. This morning when our bus went through the city it seemed as if we were driving through a war zone. Everywhere buildings were in the process of either being put up or pulled down. The 'ancient city looked every day of her 2,351 years. She was cracked, crusty and way past her prime. Yet, the adage that "beauty is only skin-deep" is true for cities too, and a few rough edges should never deter any traveler.

Upon my tour's return to the port, I leave the luxury of the *Vistaflord*, descend the gangway and head for the lights of Alexandria. I agree with Kara, our bus tour guide, that "If you wish to experience Egypt you must go to her. She will not come to you." Her words struck me as both seductive and challenging.

I accept the challenge, walk through the gates to the port and immediately I am set upon by a horse and carriage driver.

"Mister, mister! I take you to Alexandria."

"How much?"

"Ten dollars."

"Too much," I say and keep walking.

"Okay, Okay," he says with a shrug of his shoulders and side to side shake of his head, "Five dollars."

I climb into the carriage and settle into the surprising luxury of soft leather seats as we clippity-clop to the city's center.

Alexandria looks better at night. The night-lights soften her features. The dust and dirt are hidden in the shadows and the city seems cloaked in a veil of mystery. Music strange to my ears fills the night. Under a string of bare-bulb lights, I can see buyers and sellers at an outdoor market haggling. Their hands flutter like moths hovering near a candle's flame. Surely, someone will get burnt tonight.

A festive atmosphere prevails along the Corniche, the seaside promenade. The sidewalks are thick with people. Salesmen hawk their goods and couples strut their stuff. The cafes are doing a brisk business. Egyptian men loiter at outdoor tables smoking a *nargila,* a Middle Eastern water pipe, sipping strong Arabic coffee and watching the passing parade of which I have become a part. It is noisy and crowded, but not threatening. "Egyptians are friendly," Kara had told us. "Don't be surprised if they walk up and talk to you."

Indeed, I am consulting my Lonely Planet guide in search of a dining suggestion when a tall young man approaches me with a smile.

"Can I help you, sir?"

"I'm looking for the Sheikh Ali Bar."

"Are you looking for something to eat?"

"Yes or maybe just a beer."

"I know a place where you can have both."

Okay, okay. I know that in certain countries touts bring tourists to shops and restaurants where they get a commission on what the tourist buys. And I know that I should beware of strangers bearing gifts, even if they're Egyptian instead of Greek. So I say, "No, thanks," and start off. But, then I stop. What am I afraid of? I'm here to have an experience. Shouldn't I take a risk?

His name is Ali and his recommendation is just up the street. We enter a clean, well-lighted place, which advertises "pizza" and "falafel." I order two beers, but nothing else — I am cautious. But then at the next table I hear English spoken and relax. Maybe Ali is on the level.

Things proceed nicely. The beers are cold and although Ali doesn't speak much English, the people at the next table do. I strike up a conversation and discover that Mareya is an Egyptian-American who teaches at the American Cultural Center and Kareem, who was born in Alexandria, was once her student. They offer to give me an inside view of Alexandria the next day. As we talk, Ali just sips his beer, smiles and says little.

After arranging tomorrow's rendezvous spot, my new friends leave and it's time to make a decision about Ali. Considering the fact that I've met Mareya and Kareem because of him, I feel I owe him a meal.

"Let's go to the Sheikh Ali Bar," I suggest, consulting my guidebook again.

"Yes," he says. "Come, I will show you."

We hop a cab to the restaurant and as we approach the entrance Ali says, "Let me order so that they do not charge you tourist prices."

I like this place. The Sheikh Ali is frequented by locals and foreigners. It harkens back to English colonial days with an ornately designed tin ceiling and fans rotating slowly above our heads. Ali orders two large beers and a plate of squid swimming in a tomato-based sauce and a platter of peeled, boiled shrimp. The food is delicious, and is served with a plate of *tahini*, a sauce made from crushed sesame seed paste spiced with oil, garlic and lemon juice.

Dinner over, Ali negotiates payment with the waiter in Arabic. Sure, I'm suspicious when he reports that the bill seems a bit exorbitant, but I don't care if he may have tacked a few dollars on for himself.

"Now, we should go for dessert and coffee," I say. "But first I need to change money."

"I can change your money," he offers.

"Fine," I say, and give him twenty dollars.

"But I can't do it here," he says as he pockets my cash, "We have to go to shop to change it."

Once at the shop, Ali tells me to "wait" while he changes the money. But he doesn't go into the shop. Instead he walks down the other side of the street away from me. I follow. The faster he walks, the faster I walk. We must look like the Marx Brothers heading down the street one behind the other in perfect unison.

"Ali," I finally shout, "What's up?"

At my shout, he stops and comes back to me.

"The shop was closed," he says, "You wish to go to a cafe, right? We can change money there."

Finally I've had enough. "Why don't you just give me back my money?"

"Joe, Joe, please," he says, as he hails a cab. "It's okay, it's okay."

When we reach the cafe he enters the front door, and I follow. He exits out the back door, and I follow. Now standing in an alley I shout, "Ali, where are you going?"

"Stay here," he says. "I change money." For a brief second I believe him and pause. In that moment he turns the corner and is gone. I stand there alone in the alley feeling silly. And embarrassed. And then, I shrug my shoulders.

I've been scammed for food, drinks and twenty dollars. And what did I get? I met two gracious Egyptians who will give me a personal tour of Alexandria the next day and I had an experience. Not an altogether nice one, but an experience.

The night before at the ship's casino I wagered $20 at the black jack table and won $50. I had intended to go back tonight. Instead I risked $20 on a human being.

Well, as every gambler knows, sometimes you win and sometimes you lose.

Eldorado

My wife says I'm afflicted with FOMO, Fear Of Missing Out. I could argue that it's my job to be informed, to investigate everything and report on what I find. I may be right, but that doesn't make her wrong. Still, because of my uncontrollable urge to find out what that other restaurant looks like, what's around the next corner, over the next hill or where the good times roll, I have discovered amazing things and had wonderful adventures. My traveler's curiosity, which some say sits on the obsessive-compulsive end of the spectrum, has opened many doors to unexpected encounters. Then again, while I propose we practice everything in moderation, including excess, my extreme attachment to FOMO has also led me down some rabbit holes, which instead of enhancing my experience has detracted from it. But then, if you never, ever go, you never, never know.

Gaily bedight,
A gallant knight,
In sunshine and in shadow,
Had journeyed long,
Singing a song,
In search of Eldorado...

> *And, as his strength*
> *Failed him at length,*
> *He met a pilgrim shadow —*
> *'Shadow,' said he,*
> *'Where can it be —*
> *This land of Eldorado?"*
>
> *'Over the Mountains*
> *Of the Moon,*
> *Down the Valley of the Shadow,*
> *Ride, boldly ride,'*
> *The shade replied —*
> *'If you seek for Eldorado!'*

Edgar Allan Poe

Even with its modern-day restaurants, cafes, bakeries and souvenir shops, the walled city of Carcassonne, France is a knight-in-shining-armor dream come true. With its 3rd- and 4th-century ramparts and Chateau Comtal, visions of Guinevere and Lancelot dance in your head. It was here, in this Arthurian setting, that I was entrusted with a quest.

My search for the holy platter was thrust upon me as I waited behind a truck that was blocking the entrance to the narrow labyrinthine streets that led to my hotel. I sat in my rented Peugeot in the castle's shade deciding whether or not to snatch a parking space assigned to another hotel. Opting for the bold gesture, I commandeered the space. Out of the corner of my eye, I spied a figure standing in the doorway of an antique shop watching me. Climbing into my American nonchalance, I crawled out of the car and walked up to him.

"Parlez-vous l'anglais?" I asked. He nodded sage-like.

"Excusez-moi, but can I park in that space or is it reserved for the hotel?"

"No, *monsieur* — it is not reserved for the hotel."

"Great!" I said, turning on my heels.

A long thin arm reached out; tapered fingers held my shoulder. "But — *monsieur* — you can most certainly *not* park there. That space is reserved for residents of Carcassonne."

"Residents? You mean people actually live here?" a prospect that I assumed must be closely akin to taking up housekeeping in Snow White's Castle.

"Most certainly," the figure replied. "There are more than three hundred of us who live within the walls of Carcassonne."

"What's that like?"

"Very crowded and busy during the summer tourist season, but magical the rest of the year."

I must have looked a bit dubious because he added, "I also have a home on the *Méditerranée.* Do you know the *Méditerranée?"*

"Oh, yes," I enthusiastically replied. "We just came from there — we were in Collioure."

"Oh yes," he smiled, "Collioure is very nice. But, I prefer Bages."

He then drew himself up to his considerable

height (which was exaggerated by his remarkable thinness) and looked me in the eye. He bent slightly at the waist, leaned forward and in a conspiratorial whisper said, "Do not miss Bages."

"The sun never burns in Bages, it gently warms the air and the sea breezes cool the land. In Bages, the soil, climate and vines create a sweet wine, Bandol, which is the nectar of the gods. In Bages, flocks of wild flamingos wander through my front yard and — (he paused, reluctant to go on) — Do you know good food?"

"I think so."

"Well, then in Bages you may dine at Le Portanel — the finest seafood restaurant in France. There you will dine upon fish caught in a true fisherman's village and prepared by a true chef, Didier Marty. Do not miss Bages, my friend."

The words struck my ear like the clapper in a crystal bell. *Ding!* "Did he say the *best* seafood restaurant in France?" *Ding!* "Did he say *wild* flamingos?" *Ding!* "Did he say *nectar of the gods?*"

In the last three days, we had already had two of the greatest meals of my life. At La Terrasse au Soleil near Céret we had dined on a *soufflé au foie gras* and *médallion de roseé de veau des Pyrénées*. At the Auberge du Vigneron in Cucugnan we had sampled Chef Fannoy's duck specialties. Even so, Bages promised to be the shining star in a veritable celestial sea of sparkling culinary adventures. I lusted to add this jewel to my gastronomic treasure chest.

Never mind that our journalistic itinerary was filled to overflowing. If we left Carcassonne bright and early and cut short our obligatory visit to the town of Minerve, I could dash south and capture the crown before we had to be in Béziers to catch our barge cruise on the Canal du Midi. I handed my oracle my map. He circled Bages and scratched "Le Portanel" on the Mediterranean. I thanked him profusely and bid him adieu. I climbed back into my trusty steed and blessed the powers-that-be that the truck had blocked my path. Imagine if I had missed Bages.

That night my wife and I stayed within the walled city and dined at Brasserie du Donjon. As a precursor of what was to come, the manager Madam Andrée Loutrein and the wizard of our meal, Chef Eric Bivent, rolled out the culinary red carpet. We dined on *confit de canard* and *cassoulet*, drank great vintages of local wines and savored the fragrant aperitif, *Muscat de Rivesaltes*, and the port-like desert wine of *Banyuls*. Yet no matter what delectable delicacies they presented to us, and there were many, I knew this night was a mere shadow compared to the lunch that awaited us.

After dinner, Chef Bivent and Madam Loutrein opened a bottle of *Crémant de Limoux* (a slightly sparkling wine that passes excellently well as champagne). I shared with them my encounter with my shadowy benefactor and my vision of the following day. In unison they said, "Do not miss Bages."

The next morning we fled Carcassonne in the

direction of Minerve for our prearranged meeting. In my heart of hearts, I hoped that Minerve would be an ugly industrial center and the people boorish and boring. My hopes were crushed.

The village of Minerve sits perched high on a massive wedge of rock. The rivers Cesse and Brian have cut gorges out of the high plateau and in fact, the rivers have cut a 150-foot high natural cave under Minerve — yes, a river runs through it. Our hosts were warm, gracious, friendly, enthusiastic and anxious to please. They loved their town and their passions. For the teddy bear-like Monsieur J. Claude Gagnac it was the town's Archeological Museum of which he is the director and for sleek Monsieur Pascal Bourgogne it was his ancient Citroën deux chevaux and his even more historic La Bastide des Aliberts up on the hill. Immigrants from Paris, he and his wife Monique had turned a 12th Century derelict into five modern apartments for rent by the week and filled with all the comforts of home.

We ran through Minerve relentlessly dragging J. Claude and Pascal up and down the narrow streets so that I could fulfill my obligation without missing my desire. Meanwhile, it was becoming difficult to stay committed to my quest. The brilliant day, the lovely town and the warm-hearted generous Minervois were distracting me.

Our final stop was a quick visit to Pascal's les Aliberts. Home was never like this. Their backyard abutted a vineyard and from there, you could see miles and miles of the Minervois wine region, one of a multitude in Languedoc-Roussillon. We were sitting in the midst of an expanse of vineyards that were putting forth their springtime greenery. It was gorgeous.

Enjoying the wine and *joie de vivre* of the Minervois with Pascal (1997)

Monique brought out a plate of local cheeses, olives and meats and Pascal opened the bottle of Minervois cabernet. For the first time since it was mentioned, Bages was beginning to fade from my mind and I could see my wife hadn't given it a thought in ages.

The birds were hitting their sweetest notes, the family dogs were making friends big time and the sun was warming our souls. I had just about come to the conclusion that there was no better there than here. That's when Monique mentioned Bages.

Yes, Chef Marty was spectacular; in fact, he had cooked here for a special party. And the fishing village was darling. "Don't miss Bages," she said.

I came out of my chair as if I had been shot out of a cannon. We must leave, now! I couldn't miss Bages! Of course, by now we had spent so much time being seduced by Minerve that there was hardly time to get to Bages and take a spin around the block — much less eat.

No matter, I would not be deterred. I was in the grip of a frantic determination to reach Bages and have that lunch. Never mind that we were full on the treats that Pascal and Monique had laid out for us — food no longer mattered. If I did not get to heavenly Bages I would be in hell because I would have also lost the moment in Minerve.

We pulled into Bages dust flying. It was sunny and the smell of the sea was in the air — but although we had seen signs for the restaurant, it was nowhere in sight. I darted through the narrow streets until I discovered a flight of stairs that led to their door. It was lovely inside. From the upstairs dining room you looked out on the lagoon and the sea beyond. The minute we sat down I knew that I had made *une grosse* mistake.

Years ago on a press trip to the Alsace a few writers in our group complained about the time we were taking for meals. It was February, the Alsace was shrouded in fog and the air was bitter cold, but nevertheless they were tired of spending so much time feasting — they wanted to sightsee.

"There's nothing to see," I scoffed, after a typical six-course, seven-wine, four-hour lunch. "Enjoy yourself — Alsace is in here."

Still they persisted and went so far as to have our guide ask the *maitre d'* at the famous Valentin Sorg Restaurant in Strasbourg if we could do lunch in an hour.

"*C'est impossible,*" he scolded. "*C'est impossible.*"

I had snickered at the gaucherie of my fellows, but, what goes around comes around, and here I sat in one of the finest restaurants in France expecting to have a gourmet lunch in thirty minutes.

Even so, I still ordered the *daurade* encrusted in clay — and checked my watch again. My wife smiled, shook her head and ordered a plateful of *sorbets*. Pointing out what a fool I was being would have rubbed salt in my wounds and not made a bit of difference.

I got the full treatment. First they showed me the uncooked *daurade* — it was so fresh you could feel the sea spray.

"*Oui, Oui,*" I said. "Get on with it," I thought.

Time was speeding by and our rendezvous with the barge in Béziers was getting closer. Then they presented the *daurade* in a freshly prepared earthenware crust for baking.

Moments ticked away. It was hopeless. I decided to pay the bill and leave without eating.

I tried to explain to the waitress. She spoke little English. I pulled out my phrasebook and by hunting and pointing I pieced together a sentence, "Help, I need be Béziers for boat ten watch ticks past."

It worked. A look of unbelief crossed her face. I could hear her thinking, *"Crazy Americain."* Instead, she said something I knew, *"tout de suite"* — immediately. I assumed my fish was on the way.

Within two minutes, I had the *daurade* on my plate. I gave the fish a glance — it's all I had time for — it was beautifully presented. I gave it a whiff — I had no time for inhaling — the aroma was heavenly. I dove in — I had no time for savoring.

As it breezed past my lips, I felt the clean lightness in preparation. As it slid by my tongue, I tasted its natural sweetness. As it slipped down my throat, I knew that if it had the time to do so, it would melt in my mouth. Five minutes and thirty-two seconds after I started, I was finished. It was the most expensive fast food I had ever inhaled — for a brief sensual encounter that was fast becoming a bittersweet distant memory.

When the waitress brought me the check she valiantly struggled to not raise an eyebrow at my rapid conspicuous consumption.

"Merci, monsieur," she said politely.

"Pardon," I replied.

"Pas de problème, monsieur," she consoled. No problem.

I wanted to say I was sorry, I wanted to say that I

felt like a fool, I wanted to say I knew I'd insulted the chef — but I didn't have the words. Instead I just grinned like an idiot, bowed my head and slinked out the door before the chef came after me with a cleaver.

With the *daurade* trying to make itself comfortable in my stomach, we jumped into the car and rushed to the barge at breakneck speed. After stopping several times, running up to people, and yelling, "Canal du Midi? Canal du Midi?" We arrived at the dock just as our barge was heading down the canal. I leaped from the car and ran along the dock yelling after it.

The people onboard just pointed at me and stared. A crewmember pointed to the lock up ahead. I got the picture. The boat moves so slowly and the locks are so small, we could hop onboard once it entered the first lock.

Later, as the French countryside drifted by and I was calm enough to speak to, my wife, who had been extraordinarily restrained, sat next to me.

I pretended to be engrossed in a church visible in the distance. "15th century. An excellent example of the neo-gothic influence of the Italian renaissance," I muttered.

"You're amazing," she said. I could hear the smile on her face, but I refused to look at her. "Just amazing," she repeated, raising my face with her index finger.

"What do you mean," I replied, wide-eyed.

"I love you, but you're amazing," she laughed. "In mad pursuit of one experience you destroy three. That's quite a talent."

She didn't understand my plight. I had been on a fevered quest to find Eldorado — the mythical perfect somewhere that is always *"Over the Mountains of the Moon, down the Valley of the Shadow"* — just out of reach. But she was right — by reaching for the unattainable, I lost the attainable.

But I learn fast. The next day we met with Frederic Pascal and Catherine Benevois who took us to the bull-raising farm at Domaine de la Batisse for a typical Languedoc lunch. We had other people to meet and another wonderful place to be — the ancient Roman city of Nimes — but this time I did not stir until the moment at hand came to its natural end. I was unwilling to give up the riches I had for the gold I was promised.

It's good to know that if you live long enough, life gives you another chance to recognize Eldorado.

L.A.

In 1968, I came to Los Angeles to join UCLA's Master of Fine Arts program. I came with $550, which was enough for one semester's out-of-state tuition. In order to make it, I lived with a family in Holmby Hills, adjacent to the university, where, for room and board, I fluffed up pillows, vacuumed the carpets and set the Friday night Shabbat table. The Benenfelds made it possible for me to stay long enough to win a fellowship. I had applied and thanks to my father earning just $5,200 a year as a custodian, the next semester I left my new home and moved into a shared apartment. When I first came to Los Angeles I hated it. It was smoggy, traffic was bad and I didn't know anyone, so I planned to stay two years,  *pick up my degree and then move to New York and work as an actor. I did go to New York, but I've lived in Los*

51

Angeles for 52 years. The smog is better now, the traffic is worse, but like Randy Newman, I Love L.A.

I love Big Cities. I know they have problems like crime, pollution, traffic — people. But then that's why I love them — because the majority of the people in the world live in them.

And although people are not always lovable, they are hardly ever boring.

They're the best attraction going. They're better than the Eiffel Tower or the Tower of London or the Watts Towers — which are just decorations really, glass baubles on a Christmas tree; the people are the tree, the branches, the trunk and the sap that runs through the city and makes it alive.

You can't tell a city's story without its cast of characters. Without its characters, a city is like an empty movie set. Take Los Angeles. It takes a writer the likes of Raymond Chandler to bring it to life.

Ah, to write like Raymond Chandler. To make the words sing, to make them spell out the feelings that lie on the surface and the ones that are just out of reach.

To paint a picture as hard-bitten and cool and clear as a slab of ice on a hot day. To make that ice melt gently and sweetly, slowly revealing the speck of truth that makes up its center. Like Chandler did.

I wish I could capture the moment in a handful of short, bright words. Words that are unexpected, words that bite back. Words that make it good and clean and fun to be alive even in a town as mealy-mouthed and hard-nosed (Yes, I know they're opposites) as Los Angeles.

Los Angeles. Who could tell it better than Chandler. Take one down and out, slightly rumpled private detective with a name like Marlowe and set his slightly boozed-over eyes firmly staring at the smoggy Los Angeles skyline. Cool and detached, sentimental and sweet, a tough guy with a soft belly and a softer heart. A guy with a wish or two of his own. Add a generous dash of dreams and heartaches — unknown, hidden, unadmitted — and you have the perfect voice for L.A.

L.A., not Los Angeles. Los Angeles is too poetic, too Spanish, too pure and hopeful. L.A. says it all. That there's no time to say it all, so just shorten it, get it down to its essentials — if you can.

Maybe that's the challenge, to tackle the space: take the freeways, take the cars, take the people and squeeze them all down into two easy-to-write, easy-to-say letters.

Condense it, don't spend time on it; it means nothing more than it says — The Angels.

It's been done before. The Spanish called it *Nuestra Señora La Reina de Los Angeles* and the Gringos shortened it to Los Angeles. Probably because it made it more like themselves — something somebody's always trying to do.

So, we have L.A., the city everyone loves to hate. The city that seems as simple and empty as two little letters with a couple of periods.

But that's not the way it is. It just seems that way.

There's more to the city than how you spell it or what lies under the Hollywood Sign. It's everybody's idea of the American Dream stuck between the mountains and the sea. It's every possible variation on the theme that you can have what you want as long as you earn it, no matter how you earn it.

Whether it's by strutting in front of a camera or by putting in forty long boring ones, there's no glory in the work; the work's only a means to an end, and that end is the dream or the end of the dream.

There's not much of the pure sweet cleansing wash of the effort. Too often the effort is wasted, and you just end up looking at the ocean for consolation. It's the one relief from the face of repetition or failure.

The ocean reaches up onto the beach and pulls the refuse of the land into its belly. Eventually it may throw it all back up again, but it comes back changed. A little bit cleaner and softer, with the edges worn smooth.

That's what the ocean does to L.A. It softens the blows, eases the pain, modifies the harsh reality of the day-to-day and makes it possible to set one foot in front of another for another day.

Anyway, that's the way Marlowe might have seen it and that's the way Chandler might have told it. L.A. — an unimpressed, yet not necessarily uncaring city. A place for sinning and winning and losing — and a place for dreaming. A place where dreams do not always come true, but where you can always pretend they will.

A Tale of Two Cities

In 1968 I went to Los Angeles because Michael Keenan, a professional actor I met at the Asolo Theater in Sarasota, Florida, told me I'd "do well" there. I was a theater major at Florida State University doing my Equity apprentice time at the Asolo and about to graduate. As a stage actor I knew I was destined to go to New York, live in a one-room hovel and perform plays Off or Off-Off-Broadway until I made it big, i.e. got paid to act. Instead I applied to the Master of Fine Arts program at UCLA. I've never regretted that decision, but everybody knows New York is a hell of a town and if you can make it there you can make it anywhere. So, I lived in Los Angeles, but yearned for New York. In 1972, and again in 1980, I went to New York to check out living there. I interviewed my actor friends and got a sense of the life. It became clear that town was a little bit too rugged for me. It seemed New York had all the problems of Los Angeles crammed into a more compact space. Yes, it was one of the most exciting cities in the world, but one from which you can't get away. I felt my frenetic energy and The City's high-octane pace would collide and I would self-combust. So, I love New York, but I live in L.A.

Jos

This is a tale of two cities. I live in Los Angeles and I love it. But, I'm particularly fond of New York.

First of all, New York is the easiest city in the world in which to do an "on-location" radio interview. All you have to do is take out a microphone and you have a dozen people ready and willing to talk to you. And they all have something interesting to say, or if not, they're interesting themselves. Why, even New Yorkers who won't talk with you will talk with you.

One night, I approached a reluctant policeman in Greenwich Village with my microphone in hand seeking his perspective on life in the Village.

"I do no interviews," he said, "I'm not an official spokesman."

"I just wanted to ask you what's it like to be on patrol in the Village?"

"Sorry, I can't talk with you," he said emphatically, "but — if I could talk to you, I'd tell you that the Village is the friendliest place in New York. I'd tell you that the Village is the safest place in New York, and that the people are the warmest. Why, just yesterday I was telling my partner Frank ... ."

Fifteen minutes later, I had to peel both myself and "Mr. Mic" away from him.

"Thanks, officer, but I must be going now."

"Just remember," he said, practically grabbing

me by the lapels, "the Village is the best." He then paused, lowered his voice and said, "But don't tell anyone I told you so."

More often than not, when I do an interview in New York, I end up being interviewed. I get queries such as:

"Where ya from?"

"Whatcha doing?"

"What kind of a travel show, for whom and for what reason?"

Although New Yorkers are famous for being aloof, their protective shield is only aluminum foil thin. They love to get involved in your life. And that's especially true if you're in love.

I've been lucky enough to be in New York and in love twice. It is a magical experience because it's such a public celebration. If you're in love in Los Angeles, it's a secret — nobody notices — but in New York they won't let you hide it. Buy a rose for your sweetheart and New Yorkers applaud; look into each other's eyes and they sigh; kiss and they smile. Perfect strangers talk to you, offer advice, buy you things.

"Make sure he treats you right, honey!"

"Be good to that girl, she's a beauty."

"How about a drink on the house?"

"Stay in love — it's wonderful."

I'm not sure why New Yorkers are like this. Perhaps because it's a romantic city — a city of cafes, flower stalls, jazz clubs and cozy eateries. Perhaps because it's a tough city — a city where it's a relief to see the joy of others. Perhaps because it's a larger-than-life city — a monumental city, home to Rockefeller Center, the Statue of Liberty and the Empire State building. Under the skyscrapers and surrounded by the grand palaces of the industrial, financial and artistic kings and queens of America, lovers can feel like princes and princesses themselves.

New York is a city of lovers, a city filled with the ardent-hearted. In *All the Pretty Horses*, author Cormac McCarthy describes his lead character in this fashion: "All of his leanings, and all of his feelings were always for the ardent-hearted — it had always been so and would always be so."

The ardent-hearted — people enthusiastic about and for life. In Los Angeles, we live in our cars isolated behind glass and steel, separated from each other by a car length. In New York, people are crammed right up next to each other in buses, subways, theaters — well, everywhere. In Los Angeles we have plenty of space — and plenty of privacy. In New York there is no space, so you become part of the experience whether you like it or not. In Los Angeles we use our cars and our space to keep apart from others, desensitized to their life, joy and pain.

Let's try to fall a little out of love with ourselves and a little more in love with life and other people. Let's lower our car windows, open the doors, and step outside. Let's notice who's in the next car and who lives next door. Let's join the ranks of the ardent-hearted. Let's remember we're part of the human race, not part of our vehicle.

Endless Spring

I've lived my life in endless summer. I escaped Southern Florida when I was 21 and moved to Southern California. Both areas have average temperatures over 70 degrees and more than 250 days of sunshine. People invariably feel sorry for me and compelled to share the glories of "living with the seasons." I understand the attraction. Fortunately, my travels have given me the opportunity to witness all the seasons — over and over again. I've traveled up and down the hemispheres enjoying summertime snow skiing in

Taking a break among the wildflowers on a springtime
hike in Switzerland (1994)

Chile, skin-diving in winter in Fiji and followed the leaf changes from Melbourne, Australia to Sault Saint Marie, Canada. Yet, my most memorable seasonal experience was my year of springs.

It was a year of endless spring when my travels pursued the season through Europe and South America.

My springtime gambols began in March on the French Riviera. In Nice and St. Tropez springtime was a quiet time. A few hearty souls lay on the beach coaxing a tan from the sun, several braved the chilly water, but the crowds of summer were still just a memory.

From St. Tropez I drove through the wine country of Provence. Few places are lovelier than a wine country in summer when the fields are a deep green and the vines are heavy with fruit.

In the spring, before the foliage has returned, the wine country offers a stark contrast. The hills are barren and leafless; the vines a jumble of twigs. It takes faith to believe that from these pencil-thin sticks will come a great French wine.

Near Grasse, I stopped my car and walked into a vineyard for a closer look. In the swollen buds ready to burst into bloom the promise was visible.

In April, I went to Switzerland for the reopening of  the Chapel Bridge in Lucerne, a visit to Zermatt and then on to Lake Geneva. Along the grand promenade in Montreux the canopy of trees was starting to fill in and people, restless after winter hibernation, insisted upon dining *al fresco.*

But it was spring, and the sun only teased. It made an appearance once, but only lingered long enough to tantalize me with coming attractions.

At the end of May, I went to Denmark. By now, southern Europe was enjoying summer, but I continued my love affair with spring.

Copenhagen was unpredictable, one day cool and wet, the next hot. On my drive north of Copenhagen, summer arrived in all its glory, only to retreat back into spring the next day. Although for that day, Denmark was more than beautiful, it was breathtaking — a multitude of flowers in a full palate of hues, a sky so blue that it caused me to squint — and with *hyggelig* (cozy) cafés, bars and restaurants in which to warm yourself along the way.

Just when I thought I had seen the year's last spring, in September I packed my bags for Uruguay in South America. *Déjà vu.* I was transported back to bare branches, brisk breezes, lonely beaches and the promise of summer. The chic cafes of Punta Del Este were closed, but on Sunday they opened and the locals arrived in droves, as if with their arrival, summer must follow. It almost worked. At least, their smiles made me feel as warm as if I were on a beach in Mexico.

A year of springtime. As pleasant as it sounds, it was frustrating to live in a state of expectation and anticipation. Summer was foretold time and time again, but still would not arrive. I discovered spring is delightful because, "April is a promise, that May is bound to keep."

Spring is the season of possibilities, an assurance of better things to come. A season where we realize that although our wine glass is not yet filled, our fields will bear fruit.

Not unlike life. We struggle through the dark winter days of doubt, sustained by the hope that the days will get brighter, and the seeds we planted will flower. Our spring does not bring the fulfillment of our dreams, but signs that they will come true. Our spring is the time to revive our dreams and prepare to reap what we have sown.

Summer may be my favorite season, but now spring holds new pleasures for me. To see the inexorable unfurling of a new leaf on a tree, the seedling forcing its way through the soil, the drops of melting snow growing into a torrential river, is life affirming. Unconscious of any possibility that it may fail, and without fear, nature struggles to fulfill its potential.

"Knowing trees, I understand the meaning of patience. Knowing grass, I can appreciate persistence," said American journalist and naturalist Hal Borland.

Our dreams will come to fruition. Struggle and dreams are eternal. Hope and spring are essential, in order for our summer days to arrive.

The Thrill of Travel — Again

"The only thing better than being rich is traveling as if you were," said travel writer Steven Birnbaum. As a travel journalist for 40 years I've been able to have the kind of experiences he is describing and so, yes, I do indeed have a heavenly and blessed life. Yet, sometimes traveling with a mission steals from you the real reason to travel, which is to be in joy in the moment. Fifty years after my first trip abroad I still seek and treasure those times when I feel once again the thrill of the first time.

I'm excited. I'm truly excited. It reminds me of the first time I returned to Europe. Not the first time I went, because then I didn't know what to expect — but the second time, after I'd had a taste of Europe.

It's interesting that only after you've savored real pleasure do you hunger for it. Like being in love. You may want to fall in love because of what others have told you it would be like, but until you have experienced it yourself, you do not search for it and yearn for it in the same way.

So, this trip to the Midi-Pyrénées region of France feels more like my second trip to Europe. I have an excitement and expectation that I have not felt in a long time. Perhaps, like love, travel, when it becomes too commonplace, when it loses the freshness, when it loses the magic, it becomes mundane and routine, dry and lifeless.

Not this time. And I'm trying to figure out why.

Perhaps, it is because it has been a while since our last trip abroad. And like with love, absence makes the heart grow fonder. Or it could be that this time I am really trying to *parle Français*? This time I am trying to communicate with more than just hand signals and French monosyllables. I'm making an effort to understand and become an insider like never before. Is that what "love experts" call "making a commitment?"

Perhaps, it is because I am visiting the Midi-Pyrénées region of France, which, although it is new to me, strikes some familiar notes. As part of our journey, I will be visiting in Pau with a pal of thirty-plus years and become reacquainted with friends we made last year in Minerve. There is something familiar and comforting about that, without being "same old, same old" in any way.

Perhaps, it is because life has suddenly turned difficult. With the growth and changes in our lives, we have been confronted with new challenges that frighten, no, petrify us, and at times cause us to rail at each other as we cling together for dear life. The unpredictable nature of our day-to-day existence is somehow wiped away by the certainty of our European joys and pleasures. From time immemorial, this is what travelers have sought — an escape from themselves and their life.

Yet, travel is my life. So, perhaps the excitement comes from my wife who dreams of renewing our not-yet-year-old vows in a small medieval church in the village of Minerve where our new friends live and from which she was untimely ripped by me last year. Her dream will not be denied and last August at our Los Angeles wedding, I discovered that making her dreams come true excites me and that by giving to her I give to myself.

So, I can't be sure exactly from whence cometh my excitement. But the over-cooked filet mignon served on the plane tastes delightful, the Parisian flight attendant is seductive and the purser  from Nice is a *bon vivant*. They indulge my dastardly French, they feed my fantasy and tonight my love and I are on the French Riviera in a three-star Michelin restaurant eating *foie gras* and drinking Chateau Margaux 1945.

The roar of the engines as the plane cuts through the night reminds me that we are leaving behind the neurotic realities of the New World and preparing to embrace an Old World peace that age and knowledge brings.

What a relief! To shed my environment and myself and mix with a world that has existed for eons. To walk in beauty with eyes feasting on ancient stones and attempt to absorb their stories. To sense the presence of those who have walked here before me and to know that I gain something dear by being near. To dine with a love of food and drink that can be expressed without apology or restraint.

Joie de Vivre — The Joy of Life — the French have it, it is their heritage — and tonight on this trip through space, one of hundreds I have taken, I have it too!

Visions in the B.V.I.

*I feel travel should be an adventure filled with surprising
and unexpected experiences. The smallest hiccup in our
plans can become an opportunity to be creative. The chance
may crop up when we least expect it and in a way we never
imagined. I try to hang on for the ride and if it isn't exactly
pleasant, at least I can learn from it. I never know where
these serendipitous happenings may take me.*

On Virgin Gorda in the British Virgin Islands
there is a place called "The Baths." It is described in
the guidebooks as, "The premier tourist site in the
B.V.I. where huge granite boulders the size of houses
topple over one another above underlying grottos of
crystal clear water."

It is otherworldly. It is a
watery moonscape of boul-
ders poking through a tur-
quoise sea like stone icebergs.
And, as with icebergs, the
greatest mass of these granite blocks lies underwater. On
the surface they look like mini-pyramids in an aquatic
Valley of the Kings.

I've squirmed my way through the grottos to a secluded cove. I can hear the voices of my fellow "moonwalkers" in other coves — but they cannot see me nor I them. The sky is a brilliant blue, the sun is warm, but does not burn; the water is perfect — refreshingly cool, though pleasant enough to float in for hours. The buoyant sea cradles me while I glide from rock to rock — a sensation more like flying than swimming.

There is only one thing wrong. In my rush to escape the racket of the group and the heat of the asphalt road above, I have left my swim mask and contact lenses in my baggage. Once I take off my glasses the beauty before me is blurred. Above the water my uncorrected vision is good for about a foot, but it's worse below the surface. The scene looks like a watercolor whose pigments have run together — each color, image and shape melds with the next.

If I give up my wish to see clearly it is quite beautiful this way. Through the visual mist I can sense the seascape before me. I can make out the outlines and shadows of the underwater canyons, valleys and mountains. I squint for clarity. But, it's been a lifetime since my eleventh birthday when I opened gifts wearing my mother's sunglasses.

I had an eye infection. "Pink Eye," they called it. My eyes watered and burned and light made them hurt. The home remedy was cold cloths, eye drops and sunglasses until "nature took its course." Nature took its course — and my 20-20 vision with it. And since they have still not developed to my satisfaction a risk-free procedure to correct myopia — I manage with glasses, contact lenses and other visual paraphernalia.

I make the best of the situation. I dive into the watercolor painting and chase a group of moving paint splotches that I assume are fish.

When I crawl up on a flat-topped rock and gaze into the water, I discover that the water's surface acts as a magnifying lens. The refraction is a near perfect fit.

I can plainly see a group of parrotfish nibbling on a particularly yummy brain coral. A long-armed yellow anemone beckons to a small purple fish — a come-on that he'd best ignore. A red-striped fellow darts in and out of the crevasses in the stones.

There is only one thing wrong. The Baths are a place to linger, but I have only minutes and they are ticking away. The press group I'm hitched to is scheduled to board a boat for Norman Island in ten minutes. So, reluctantly I swim back to the rock where I have squirreled away my things, climb up on the slippery slope and breathe in the fresh sea air.

"This is heaven," I shout out loud, an exhalation designed to shake off the rising feelings of loss.

"It is what it is," I whisper to myself. "No need to ruin the moment by demanding more."

Yet, distracted by "if onlys" and "could haves," I unthinkingly shake out my shorts and then hear a soft, "Kerplunk." Immediately I realize that "Kerplunk" is the sound of $900 worth of visual aids going into the drink.

"Oh, shit!" In this perfect place, now there's a problem. My mind is rushing — wanting to panic — but about what? About Loss. Not just loss of my specs, but of the serenity, the day, the moment. My ears fill with nagging voices.

"You jerk. Just when things are perfect, you spoil them. It's always like that."

I feel alone and helpless — unable to see.

I take a breath and jump into the water. I try to feel for my glasses, but the water seems to have risen and the calm sea now rushes in, crashes on the rock and creates a foam that's difficult to see through. Each breaking wave spells L.O.S.S.

Then a calmer voice reminds me of the parrotfish and the looking glass surface. Even with my eyes I should be able to find the glasses with a swim mask. I climb atop my rock and call out to a lady who is walking along the shore carrying a snorkel and fins.

"Hello," I shout, "I dropped my glasses. Could I use your mask to find them?"

"I haven't seen them," she says.

"I know. They're not there, they're here," I say, pointing to the foot of my rock.

"You found them?" she answers.

"They're underwater. Can I use your mask?"

"I don't have a mask," she replies.

I don't have the time to figure out why she's carrying fins and a snorkel, but no mask. The bus, the group, Norman Island are waiting. I climb from rock to rock back to land and go in search of a swim mask.

As I round a boulder I run smack into four of them. They are all perched on the heads of a family from Nebraska.

"Could I use a swim mask," I say with a tinge of desperation in my voice. "I dropped my glasses in the water."

"Sure," says the husband, "Take mine."

I do, and head back to my cove. With my underwater vision improved I dive again and again among the rocks. And finally, there, tucked in a fish hole are my spectacles. A raggedy-looking character defiantly guards the opening. He looks like a schoolyard tough. His fins are nipped and tattered from past tussles. And he's claimed my glint of gold as his own — "Finders Keepers, Losers Weepers," he seems to say as he swims out to confront me.

No moray eel, shark or barracuda, he's more of a blowfish with a puffed-up view of himself. I sweep him aside and grab my glasses. He gives way, but nips me on the hand in protest.

As I surface I hear the family calling. "Hello, there, have you found your glasses?"

"Yes," I shout back, "Thanks for your help."

"No problem," the man answers as I make my way to where they're spreading out their towels. "This is a nice spot. We're glad we ran into you." His family nods in agreement. And I feel nothing short of undying love and gratitude.

71

"You're very welcome," I say.

"Where you from?" he asks.

"Los Angeles."

"Jeez, you've come a long way to come close to losing something important, didn't you?"

"Closer and more important than you know," I reply. He nods knowingly, his wife smiles and their two little girls wave goodbye.

Back at the road, the group has left, but our tour leader is waiting for me.

"What happened?" she asks.

"I dropped my glasses, needed a mask, met nice people — but All's Well That Ends Well."

"We thought you had a heart attack."

"Oh, my life's never that simple," I reply.

Freedom to Roam

Julie and I recently returned from Cuba. It was my sixth and best visit to the island of my forefathers. In the past I've visited Havana, Matanzas, Varadero, Holguín, Santiago de Cuba, Cienfuegos, Trinidad and, of course, the province of Pinar del Rio, the birthplace of Cuban cigars and my grandfather, Carlos Lazo. I loved it! Cuba has the best scenery, the best music, the best food and the best people. This last trip we stayed five days in Viñales, the small colorful town in the middle of the beautiful Viñales Valley, a UNESCO World Heritage site since 1999. I felt I was home. The largest island in the Caribbean, I have much more of the country to see and, as a journalist,

Celebrating sunset with my wife Julie on Havana's Malecón, its seaside esplanade. The 1589 El Morro fortress shares the frame. (2020)

at least I still have the right to see it. Unfortunately, most Americans don't have that freedom to roam. As of the summer of 2020, the U.S. government has expanded the disgraceful 60-year boycott of Cuba and Americans are not legally permitted to travel on their own to Cuba. In fact, no American airline is allowed to fly to any other city in Cuba, but Havana. We can travel to Russia and China, but not Cuba. The freedom to travel is a basic American right. The U.S. Constitution tells us our creator has endowed us with the inalienable right to "Life, Liberty and the Pursuit of Happiness." If freedom to travel is not essential for happiness, I don't know what is.

Why we travel is more important than where we travel.

Of course, if you've traveled abroad you know that, as far as U.S. Customs is concerned, there are basically only two reasons why we travel: for business or pleasure. It's a question on the declaration form.

In truth, there are probably as many "whys" as there are people who travel. The poet Robert Lowell said, "The wise man travels to discover himself." The columnist Earl Wilson offered, "A vacation is what you take when you can no longer take what you've been taking."

I travel for change. Not for a change of scenery, but for a change in me. I always hope to come back different, in some way augmented by the experience.

While tourists sight-see, travelers seek people, adventures and experiences. Travelers don't scan the globe to tick off entries on a list of world wonders — Eiffel Tower, Taj Mahal, Great Wall of China — and they seek to bring back more than baubles and trinkets.

On a recent trip to Sweden and Norway, I discovered that I brought back a right — *Allemansrätten.*

It literally means "Everyman's Right." And, in essence, it is a freedom granted by their constitutions that allows anyone to picnic or pitch a tent for one night on private land without the owner's permission.

In Sweden and Norway, with rights come responsibilities. For additional night stays, it is customary to ask permission; you must leave the area as spotless as you found it and, at no time, should you infringe on the owner's *hemfridszon* — immediate living space, which is nebulously defined as the area they maintain by mowing the grass, planting flowers, putting in a garden, etc.

At first, I thought this was a quaint notion that conjured up visions of tramping through the countryside, tenting out for free in uncultivated fields unfettered by "No Trespassing" signs. It was a sweet, antiquated, naive idea that assumed trust and maturity — a true cultural eccentricity with little relevance to me. I wasn't prepared for how quickly and subtly the idea would affect me.

One day on my Gota Canal Cruise between Stockholm and Gothenburg, Sweden, we biked ahead of the boat to the next town for a picnic along the river. On the cruise you travel on a historic boat through 66 locks, one river, eight lakes and two seas.

It's a lovely trip and in many places you can walk faster than the ship moves.

While we waited for our boat, we nibbled our *ost* (cheese) and *skinka* (ham) sandwiches and drank a Class II (medium strong) beer. After a while, a family of four came up, walked through our space and sat down at the river's edge, a few feet in front of us.

They enjoyed the river, oblivious to us. Yet, what was more surprising, I was oblivious to them. The idealistic little notion of right of access had rubbed off on me. Since, in theory, I was free to share their space, I was relieved of the need to be protective and possessive of my space.

Don't worry; it's not an idea I'm transplanting to the States right away. It's taken generations for the Swedes to agree that you can trust the other guy enough to share with him — that if you give him a hand, he won't take your arm. That instead of the macho myth of rugged individualism, perhaps it's the everyday reality of communal responsibility that wins the day.

We're different. In the United States, we're obsessed with individual rights. So, we put up walls and arm ourselves to protect them.

In Sweden and Norway as well, they're concerned with all people's rights — *Allemansrätten*. Property isn't very private, and so, the boundaries between people are lifted.

So, who's freer?

As our Gota Canal adventure came to an end in

the lovely town of Gothenburg, it was the concept of *Allemansrätten* and freedom to roam that stayed with me.

It's with me still. Ownership, territory and community have taken on a new meaning. A shared space, a shared city, a shared world — one of the surprising joys I received from traveling in Scandinavia.

An Alarming Proposal

During one of my many Travelscope Taiwan television shoots, one night from outside my hotel I heard Beethoven's Für Elise playing in the distance. I couldn't imagine where it was coming from at this late hour? A night market? A street performer serenading a crowd? Was it a car radio or some neighbor's old phonograph? I left the hotel and followed the tune down dark streets and back alleys anxious to locate the founder of this musical feast. Finally, I turned a corner and there before me was the source of Beethoven's unrequited love song — a big yellow garbage truck. It's true, rather than the irritating "beep, beep, beep" that our trash trucks emit going through our neighborhoods; in Taiwan garbage trucks play Beethoven. I took in the performance, applauded loudly to the amusement of passersby and smiled to myself. Ah, here, finally, was validation of the obviously visionary Musing I had written decades before.

Los Angeles has long been considered the smog capital of the United States. Although, these days it seems even the most pristine places have pollution. Why even Yosemite Valley, the most heavenly spot on earth, suffers from auto emissions every summer. And during my last visit to San Francisco, that city by the Bay, my heart was broken as from my hotel room in the Berkeley Hills I gazed across the Bay through a familiar brown haze.

The good news is that most of us are working harder than ever to clear the skies and our lungs. In California we have adopted tough environmental and smoking laws. Yet, I'd like you to consider not what we breathe, but the pollution we hear.

No, this is not another liberal diatribe against the stuff that is blasted at us over talk radio. Although the junk dished out from bloated, blustering, blowhards is enough to make me choke, I'm talking about the everyday sounds of urban life.

Take a moment and listen.

From the cacophony of the city, there is one sound that crosses all boundaries from inner city bastions to the posh enclaves of yuppiedom to millennialville; there is one sound that overcomes leaf blowers, jack hammers, dogs barking, the child's cry and the helicopter's whirl; a noise, a racket, a din that outdoes them all — car alarms.

They come in ear-piercing, nerve-racking variations that range from a constant shriek to a pulsating wail. Some pause for a second, give us a false hope, and then go off louder than before.

Car alarms are an affront to our sensibilities and infringe on our attempts to create a fortress of solitude. Every man's home may be his castle, but car alarms can breach the stoutest stonewalls. And they don't really work.

When you hear a car alarm do you ever think, "Oh dear, someone is attempting to heist an automobile. Hurry, I must call the police."

I don't think so. I'd bet most people say, "That #@!* inconsiderate jerk. If someone is stealing that car, I hope they hurry it up and get it out of earshot."

Car alarms are worse than second-hand smoke. I can avoid a smoker, but errant car alarms affect us all. I'm sure they are bad for our health. I'd rank them up there with gluten and sugar.

They've become a part of our culture. And they're not limited to the big cities. There's probably a farmer in Nebraska with an alarm on his tractor to protect it from cartoonist Gary Larsen's cows.

Car alarms have become so much a part of my life that during a trip to the French Riviera recently I heard a "chirp, chirp, chirp," and thought it was a Mercedes. It turned out to be a real live cricket.

And yet, far be it for me to advocate any change that would cause people who manufacture alarms to lose their livelihoods. So, I propose we keep the car alarm factories open, but retool them so that they make car alarms that sound like — church bells.

That's right, church bells. When I was in Denmark recently, I realized how Europeans live with the soothing sounds of bells. Each village has a church or clock tower with sonorous bells that mark time, summon worshipers or, just for the fun of it, play Bach concertos.

If we re-tune car alarms, our neighborhoods would be filled with lovely dulcet tones. Or the alarms could be made to toll out bits of our favorite tunes — classics from Beethoven or Mozart, yes, but also Beatle songs like, "Help!" or "Baby, You Can Drive My Car," Rick Dupree's "Steal Away" or ... Well, you get the idea.

Before you laugh me off, just think of the difference it would make.

It would lift our spirits and nurture in us the goodwill to actually check on our neighbor's vehicles. Instead of repelling us, the melodies would attract us. Like the Pied Piper's children we would be drawn to the melody and form a circle around the car to protect it — and perhaps sing together. Hey, it's the 50th anniversary of Woodstock — why not have a hootenanny? And since music soothes the savage beast, my idea may stop auto thieves altogether.

So, what do you say, mister? Want to sign my petition?

Wanderlust

Time for Living
Adventure Can't Wait
The Traveling Road Show
Memories Are Made of This
Traveling Young

Time for Living

Except for the year when I bagged groceries at the local Kwik Chek grocery store in Miami, I have always worked for myself. When I graduated from UCLA with an MFA degree in theater and began to pursue an acting career I supported myself with a paper route with the Los Angeles Times and then as a door-to-door Fuller Brush Man (Google it). As a prospective actor I needed my days open to make phone calls, attend auditions, take classes and perform for free in showcase theaters. I worked the paper route from 2am to 6am every day and I made my own Fuller Brush hours. I quit the paper job after six months and although I didn't get rich as a Fuller Brush man, I did support my acting habit for fourteen years. Why didn't I just settle down and get a regular job? I was offered many: print journalist, restaurant manager, teacher, stock broker, travel agent, real estate agent, etc. I was more in love with time than money. If life came a'knockin' I wanted to be available. My travels had taught me that a two-week vacation would never be enough.

Two weeks! On an average, Americans get two-and-a-half weeks paid vacation. Most workers get a little over two weeks to rest and recuperate from an entire year of the stresses and strains of the workaday world.

It's a shame! Of all the industrialized, prosperous nations of the world, the United States is at the bottom of the heap when it comes to time off to enjoy the fruits of our labors. The French, Swedish and Germans are guaranteed a month paid vacation. In Spain and Italy they get three weeks, plus another three weeks in public holidays. And get this, mates, Aussies are entitled to four weeks off and many get five. That's time to roast quite a few shrimp on the barbie.

The workers of these nations are given the time to live their life now, not defer it until later. If you think about it, we Americans work our entire lives so we can live it up when we retire. My God, if and when we do retire, most of us won't have a lot of living left to do.

When I turned 27, I went to Europe for the second time. I had saved just enough money to spend it all on three months in Europe. On the way to the airport, I ran into my neighbor.

"Where are you going in such a rush, Joe?" he asked.

"To Europe for three months," I replied stopping in mid-stride.

A wide grin spread across his face. "That's good. That's real good," he said.

"Have you ever been," I asked.

He shook his head. "No. We always wanted to go, but never thought we could afford it."

"And now?" I asked.

"Now we've got the time and money, but we're too sick to travel," he said with an ironic laugh, "never thought about that."

"Have fun," he sighed, walking away, shaking his head. "It's all that matters."

You see, we've got it all wrong. Money is important, but there are other things more important. Not only can money not buy you love, it can't buy you time. When we're striking and fighting for better wages, we must not forget to agitate for more vacations. We can all <u>use</u> more money; we all <u>need</u> more free time.

I saw a bumper sticker the other day: "The guy who ends up with the most toys wins!" Baloney. He whose goal is collecting toys ends up working himself to death. And, you can't take your toys with you.

I say, "He who ends up with the most experiences and memories wins." Maybe I can't take them with me either, but at least they don't depreciate.

In fact, they increase in value. Just thinking about a trip brings back all the sights, smells — and feelings — as if they've just happened. Perhaps instead of always concentrating on our bank deposits we should spend more time making deposits in our memory banks.

AND struggle for more and longer vacations. Let's get in sync with the rest of the industrialized world — let's be a little less rich and a little more travel happy. For as Mozart said, "What are people... without travel, but poor creatures indeed."

Adventure Can't Wait

Webster defines anticipation as "expectant waiting." Long before I knew the definition I was an expert at it. My parents were masters of suspense equal to Alfred Hitchcock and much of my childhood was spent waiting, wishing and hoping for things to happen. I never knew for certain if what they promised would, in fact, happen. My anticipation was heightened by the possibility of disappointment. More than once holding my breath while I was "expectantly waiting" impelled me to take matters into my own hands.

I have trouble getting to the airport early. The rule of thumb is to arrive three hours before an international flight and two hours before domestic flights, but lately getting to the airport has been a travel adventure itself.

I'd like to blame the fates. My taxi was late picking me up, my alarm didn't go off, my travel agent messed up my flight times, but as Jimmy Buffet sings in *Margaritaville*, "Hell, it could be my fault." It's just hard for me to get up early these days.

Whatever the reason, I'm tired of sprinting to the gate, coat flying, heart thumping and forehead sweating. Arriving in a state of anxiety makes a real impression on airport security.

I didn't always have this problem. When I was growing up in Miami, Florida we always left early on trips.

I say trips, but I mean trip. Each summer we spent two days in Key West. My father was born there, and we made the pilgrimage once a year.

We'd start out very early in the morning. The goal was to leave while the stars were still out. "I want to beat the heat," my father would say. As for my mother, she was always obsessed with arriving and leaving early anywhere. We'd go to a family picnic and wait three

Ready to leap with brother Ron at Key West's southernmost beach (1962)

hours for the rest of the family to arrive on time. By the time they got there, my mother was ready to leave.

But whatever my parents' reasons, leaving early was okay with me. A trip offered escape and adventure, and I yearned for both.

I never slept the night before our trip. It was like Christmas for me. But instead of waiting to hear

Santa's reindeer, I was waiting for my parents' alarm clock to go off.

One year the anticipation drove me to desperation. After a night of tossing and turning, I finally gave up. I lay in bed wide-awake wondering, "Is it time, yet?" Slowly, I got out of my bed and crawled into my parents' room to check the clock.

There it was — on my father's dresser next to the glow-in-the-dark plastic statue of the Virgin Mary. It was an old clock. The glass face was broken. It had to be wound with a pair of pliers. It stopped often, but my father refused to chuck it.

"It works as good as a new one," he'd say. Well, he was almost right. The alarm did work and it kept reasonably good time, but it only ran when lying on its face.

That particular morning, I crawled alongside my parents' bed to the clock. With a deft twist of my wrist, I turned the clock over, took a look and laid it back down again. Just as I thought. The clock was set for five, but it was only four now. Another hour to wait.

"Wait a minute," I thought, "I could reset the alarm." No easy task — one false move and the clock could stop, and only my father knew the secret incantations that could get it started again.

But I had to try. By the light of the Virgin Mary, I carefully turned the alarm back to 4:15. And then just as the ticking began to slow, I quickly set it back on its face.

Back in my bed, I immediately regretted it. What if it doesn't work? If the clock stops, I could lay here for hours. What if it works? Would they guess I set it back? I could always blame my little brother. No, that wouldn't work this time; he's too young to tell time.

Uncertain of my future, I counted seconds instead of sheep. "One thousand and one, one thousand and two, one thousand and three" — about 900 thousands later the alarm went off, startling me so badly, I almost yelled out.

"Has it always been that loud?" I wondered.

Somewhere through the din, I heard my parents.

"Josie, get up!" said my mother.

"It's too early," said my father.

"The alarm has gone off."

I could hear my father stomping out of bed.

"What the ... It's only quarter past four," he said.

"You must have set the alarm wrong," she accused.

"I didn't set the alarm wrong!" His voice rising. Huddled in the sheets I held my breath and waited for the explosion.

Silence.

"I just want to make sure we beat the heat," he said proudly, and I heard drawers opening and closing as he began to dress.

And so, I survived (although, they did have a whiff of suspicion!).

We packed the old Ford station wagon with luggage, and my brother grabbed our stuffed animals. Mine was named Lucky. I had won him in a PTA raffle, and he went on those Key West vacations with me until he lost his eyes and his stuffing began to leak out.

In Key West with my mother Edalia and Ron alongside my dad's faithful Ford (1960)

As we prepared to leave, the neighborhood was quiet. Although the sky was brightening, the stars were still out. The palm trees rustled in the gentle breeze. The air felt fresh and cool. Thanks to me, we had beaten the heat.

The luxurious El Prado Motel, our one-night stop! (1962)

I still love traveling. But, I've never hungered for the escape and the promise of travel — real or imagined — more than during those journeys of my childhood. It was a snap getting up then.

The Traveling Road Show

I was an actor for 14 years before becoming a travel writer. After years of being judged on whether I was old enough, young enough, tall enough, short enough, white enough or Latin enough, being judged on my work was a relief. And the rejections were so easy. As opposed to "Don't call us, we'll call you," editors were kind and sent me well-written notes on

My 1970s Hollywood headshot

nice letterhead. While my acting career never fully blossomed, the many years of training didn't go to waste. I produced and hosted the Travelscope radio show for twenty-three and a half years and I've hosted, written and directed Joseph Rosendo's Travelscope on PBS for 12 seasons and 130 episodes. Every show is a story and each journey loaded with dramatic twists and turns, unexpected discoveries, fascinating characters and an accompanying score that's always running through my head.

Sometimes my life seems like a musical comedy — with a tune for every occasion. On some days I can 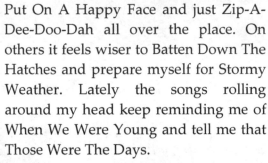 Put On A Happy Face and just Zip-A-Dee-Doo-Dah all over the place. On others it feels wiser to Batten Down The Hatches and prepare myself for Stormy Weather. Lately the songs rolling around my head keep reminding me of When We Were Young and tell me that Those Were The Days.

I'm not afraid of getting old. Although it's not a particularly pleasant prospect, I much prefer it to the only other option. And dying doesn't trouble me half as much as having never lived. Sooner or later, we're all going to be (as Dennis Miller used to say on Saturday Night Live) "Outta here!" I'd just like to make sure that I made the most of my stay.

In my youth, my friends and I promised "to gather rosebuds while we may" — *Now* was the only time, *Today* the only day. You could be hit by a truck *Tomorrow*. We knew we may be following Aesop's fabled grasshopper down a thorny path, but it suited us fine. Who wants to be a drudge ant, anyway?

So, for much longer than twenty years ago today, I figured out that since you can't really be immortal no matter how many home runs you hit, how much money you make or how many babies you have — I'd best fill my days doing something I liked.

Acquiring material things didn't seem the answer. No matter what the bumper stickers say, the guy with the most toys doesn't win; in fact, I'm pretty sure he's a loser. It's memories that find a permanent home in the recesses of our hearts and minds.

Wearing a *gho*, the national dress, at an all-day Tshechu (religious festival) in Bhutan (2012)

Once I got that idea under my belt, I sat right down and tried to figure out how to gather up some bright red, long-stemmed memories. I searched around in all the wrong and right places and came up with — if not all happy memories — a vivid bunch that will keep me occupied for a lifetime.

From my first trip to Europe with that USO road show to my recent journeys through the dzongs of Bhutan, the wats of Cambodia and the pagodas of Myanmar, I've come back stuffed with picture-postcard-clear images.

The Alpine meadows of Switzerland, the sweet surprise of a German Mosel wine, the bistros of Paris, the great serpentine wall of China, the colorful chaos of Kathmandu — places, faces and encounters indelibly etched into my mind.

Once I decided that travel was my protection against an empty memory bank, I jumped at every chance to get out of town. I traded money and security for the chance of a trip. Finally, I made it official and became a travel journalist. Now, travel is my work, and Thanks For The Memories.

So it may sound hokey, but when my thoughts turn to Yesterday I remember that now are The Good Old Days and accept as a challenge author Jonathan Swift's blessing: "May you *live* all the days of your life."

Memories Are Made of This

In 1969, as a 23-year-old graduate student in Theater at UCLA, I was cast in the then hit musical "How to Succeed in Business Without Really Trying." We were going to Europe to entertain American troops in West Germany for the USO. It was my first time out of the country and as a young man from a young country I was overwhelmed by

The 1969 UCLA/USO cast performing "Coffee Break" from *How to Succeed...* . This was the size of most army base stages. On the far right, I'm acting out caffeine withdrawal.

Europe's history, thrilled by its cultures, touched by its traditions and overjoyed by its celebrations. I was hooked. I was hooked on a dream of traveling the world discovering, learning and growing. That trip changed my life and started me on the path to be a travel journalist. In the fifty years since then I've collected a lifetime of travel memories. And although I have a reporter's recall, I sometimes wonder if I'm remembering them the way they were or the way I want them to be ... or if it matters.

Do travel experiences mellow with age like a fine wine? Does time soften the edges or sharpen them? Perhaps, like wine, it depends on the quality we put into the bottle. And, of course, it depends on the bottle.

"One always begins to forgive a place as soon as it's left behind," said English author Charles Dickens. Incidents that were frightening can become amusing with the passage of time. Earth-shattering events lose their emotional punch.

How about traveling? Does time make a trip more exciting and enlightening once we're home? Do time and distance allow us to look back and realize how rich, unique and unusual our experiences were? And, what's really important, what happened or our memory of what happened? Is there a difference?

If the bad experiences fade and the good times come into clearer focus, some say we're lucky. Others say we're just fooling ourselves. Yet, if a trip is an adventure, then even the unpleasant happenings are part of it. The worst thing must be to look back on a journey and realize it was truly "once-in-a-lifetime" (as they all are) — and that we never noticed.

Of course, it's easy not to notice. There are many things to think about on a trip. "Where do we eat? How many whatsitz are there to a dollar? Where are we going to go and what are we going to do next?"

While we spend our time fretting over what is about to happen, our trip passes us by. It would be tragic to think, "I remember Rome, that's where the bus broke down."

And while we glanced away, what passed us by? Perhaps an experience we would cherish for life. A precious moment to add to our bag of moments as children hoard perfectly clear marbles to admire in secret when they need to know something special is theirs. Travel memories can be as precious. They can stay with us for a lifetime, and keep us forever rich.

If we could slow down, and really look outside ourselves when we travel, we would not return home with an empty sadness — only the urge to travel again.

How do we manage to do it? We could train. A good traveler needs to be as fit and well-conditioned as an athlete. But we don't have to master the New York Marathon right off. We could start with small trips. A walk around the block, perhaps. We could try to see it all — really see, not just look.

"Do human beings ever realize life while they live it — every, every minute?" asks Emily in Thornton Wilder's play, *Our Town*.

"No," replies the godlike stage manager, "Saints and poets maybe — they do some."

I hope Mr. Wilder won't mind if I add us "traveling fools" to his short list.

Traveling Young

At about the time I found out that there wasn't a Santa Claus I realized that people died. It was a shocking revelation and in order to avoid the pain and loss of it, I determined that I would become my favorite Disney character, Peter Pan. Why? He never gets old and always stays a kid. In Neverland, time stands still for him. I decided that since I couldn't stop time, I'd make the most of it. I'd do everything, drink everything and eat everything. I would always speak my mind, tell people I loved that I loved them and never grow old — in spirit, anyway. I mean if tempus fugit — time flies — the only thing to do is carpe diem — seize the day.

To pass the time on a recent Delta Airlines flight, I searched through the seat pocket in front of me. Along with the emergency instruction card, the airsickness bag and a few empty packages of honey-roasted peanuts, I discovered a copy of Sky, their in-flight magazine. Idly thumbing through it, I ran across a question-and-answer column written by syndicated columnist Joel Achenbach. One of the questions was, "Why does time speed up as you get older?"

It caught my attention. I'm getting older and, considering the alternative, plan on getting much older. I'd often heard people complain about this phenomenon and had experienced it myself.

Mr. Achenbach answered, "Time is a dimension by which we subjectively try to take measure of the world. As we take this subjective measurement, two things are happening at once: We are receiving input, and then comparing it to the rest of our memories. Over time, this means life becomes less 'impressive,' because each bit of stimulus has to compete with a greater amount of memory. Life gets duller, compared to what it is like for a six-year-old. A year doesn't seem as long anymore because each passing year becomes an ever-smaller fraction of our memory. Smaller is perceived as shorter."

My first response was disappointment that the theory doesn't apply to the time spent waiting at airports. Then I decided that, although that may be because airports exist in some sort of "Twilight Zone" where time stands still, it's probably due more to the "a-watched-pot-never-boils" theory than to what Achenbach was writing about.

My second reaction was: depression. His answer made sense. The more we live, the smaller percentage each day is of our total life; so, the faster time slips by, the less of our life we live. Not a happy thought. But, after overcoming the urge to open the emergency door and really speed things up, I considered the concept.

I ended up deciding, "There must be an antidote for this insidious thievery — something we can do to slow time."

Then one of Achenbach's points struck me: "Life gets duller, compared to what it is like for a six-year-old." Why? Besides fewer memories, what does a six-year-old kid have that a seventy-something elderly fellow doesn't?

Curiosity. Fascination. Wonder. A six-year-old is experiencing everything for the first time.

Remember how long it took for Christmas morning to arrive? Or for the sun to rise before you left on vacation? Or to be kissed for the first time?

Don't get me wrong; I'm not advocating a return to childhood. Heaven forbid, I might not survive it the next time. Yet, I do prescribe that we recapture our child-like view of life.

How? By never stopping to discover and to attempt new things. It's not just a matter of perception, not just believing the "pop" poster psychology that states, "Today is the first day of the rest of your life." What if the rest of your life is as dull as ditchwater? It's a matter of actions and choices.

If we can fill our days with new experiences, then time will slow down and we will retain our youth. For what is youth, but a fresh, hopeful view of the world? What is youth, but the ability to be surprised? If we know it all, what is there to live for? An old dog must learn new tricks.

The rewards are great. If we can keep our lives alive with new ideas, emotions and challenges, the clock's heavy hands will slow so much that, when time finally runs out, we won't wonder where it all went; we'll be ready to go — exhausted from all we've accomplished and experienced.

So tomorrow is another day filled with endless possibilities — good, bad and indifferent. We'll win some, we'll lose some, and some will be called on account of rain. Sure, life is short, but don't worry, if we let the child in us breathe a bit, there's plenty of time to enjoy it.

We already know that none of us is getting out of here alive. So, the greatest tragedy is not dying; it's never having lived.

Writer Hunter S. Thompson expressed it this way, "Life should not be a journey to the grave with the intention of arriving safely in a pretty and well preserved body, but rather to skid in broadside in a cloud of smoke, thoroughly used up, totally worn out, and loudly proclaiming, "Wow! What a Ride!"

All You Need Is Love

Age Means Nothing
It Takes Two to Travel
Summertime Blessings
A Travel Romance Test

Age Means Nothing

Many of these stories were written in the 1990s and early 2000s. I've updated them a bit here and there, but left most of them in their era. I couldn't renew this one without it sounding strange. At seventy-something it's hard to write about not looking your age and I'm happily married now. Although age has never meant much to me, in our culture, it's a major descriptor. Even so, besides not trusting anyone over thirty once, I've tried not to give into the ageist prejudices and stereotypes. There are times though when la différence can't be denied.

I'm forty-something. I don't look it, I'm told. I look late thirty-something, so I don't usually mention my age. I only tell you my approximate age as a point of reference.

Don't misunderstand; I'm not keeping my age a secret because I'm embarrassed about it. I'm not embarrassed about my age, I'm proud of it. I've worked a long time getting to it. I've gone through a lot of trial and error, pain and suffering, and blood, sweat and tears. (Oops, using '60s rock and roll band references is sure to date you.)

Yet, in spite of my "I'm Aging and I'm Proud" attitude, I've learned that being in the vanguard of the Baby Boomer army that is about to descend into the flab-ulous fifties is not something to brag about — especially if you're a man living the supposedly swinging single life.

At this time of my life, I'm supposed to be married with children. It's not necessary that I be happily married, but at least married and with almost-grown children. Being married and having almost-grown children indicates a seriousness and stability that being single and childless does not. If you're male and of an age and looking for love (in all the right places, of course) women your age tend to be attracted to stability. I'm not criticizing, I understand their position — they're not getting any younger, either.

Stability is usually equated with financial health — stocks, bonds, cash, goods — anything which proves worth (those thousands spent on therapy don't really cut it). And since I followed the grasshopper's path instead of the ant's, I don't have much to show for those forty-something years. My acquisitions have been minor — a small home, a six-year-old Mazda Protege, two cats — some folks might even ask what I've been doing all my life. They wouldn't be very nice folks, though.

Even though I'm forty-something, except for occasional back pain and weak jogging knees, I feel much younger. Of course, a little mental manipulation has helped keep reality at bay. For instance, I still believe I can become anything I want (although I just removed brain surgeon from my list of possibles) and from time-to-time, I date women who could be one of my non-existent almost-grown children.

Recently I dated a woman I met at a business function. I assumed she was thirty-something, but she turned out to be early twenty-something. "Well, age means nothing," I told myself as I asked her out. It only proved my point when to my pleasant surprise, she accepted.

She arrived at the five-diamond, beachfront hotel I had chosen for a drink dressed in what I can only describe as roller-blading gear — short black spandex pants, a baggy sweater and tube top (Do they still call them tube tops?). No problem, the nice thing about Los Angeles is you can dress any way you like and no one will say anything — you might be an eccentric television star. After a drink and a chat, I suggested escaping to a quiet, unobtrusive Mexican restaurant for dinner.

Dinner was a big success. They found us a cozy booth hidden way in the back of the restaurant and we had a grand old time. The conversation was intelligent and refreshing,  the surroundings pleasant and the food was great. She loved the veggie burritos, approved of the lard-free tortillas and giggled when the water came with lemon slices. I was suggesting after-dinner coffee and congratulating myself with another "Age Means Nothing" pat on the back when I noticed a dark cloud cross her face.

"Is something wrong," I asked.

"Instead of coffee, do you really want to know what I'd like?" she asked.

"Yes, I would," I replied hopefully.

"I'd like to go for a run."

"A run?" I gulped. "It's midnight."

"Oh, I know," she joyfully replied. "But I feel so guilty about not working out tonight. Would you like to join me?"

"I wish you had mentioned it before my second cognac," I muttered.

"You don't have to come," she said, coolly.

"Oh, I'm game," I said, recovering my *savoir faire*, "Where do you want to run?'

"Oh, I don't know — somewhere near the ocean."

Now, I'm not one to be taken in by all the media fear mongering, so I actually think Los Angeles is a pretty safe place, but running on a beach after midnight is a tad foolish. Yet, young fools rush in where old men never, never go — so after a quick decision and a fast stop to pick up my running stuff (She came dressed in hers, remember?), we proceeded to jog along the beach into Marina del Rey.

I picked Marina del Rey for very sound reasons. I figured that — just in case — it was residential enough someone would hear our screams, and perhaps, even bother to come to our aid.

So off we dashed along a beach where moonbeams sparkled on the water, passed condos where lovers cuddled cozily on the sofa, by a jetty where couples sat arm-in-arm watching the flotsam head out to sea. Dogs barked at us, cats ran from us, people stared at us, cops cruised us — still, we ran on.

I'm proud to say I kept right in step with her. I puffed no harder than she did (never mind that she was a heavy smoker), and an hour later when we arrived back at my car she gave me a compliment.

"You're in great shape," she said, "… for your age."

"Thanks," I said. "So are you."

It, of course, did not work out between my twenty-something friend and me. Yet, I still think that "Age Means Nothing" — it's shared personal experiences that are important. I knew our romance was doomed the night of our mad dash. As we sprinted by a Marina del Rey record store (Are they still called record stores?) that was ballyhooing the new Beatles Anthology she shook her head and asked, "Who are those guys, anyway?"

It Takes Two to Travel

My wife Julie and I have worked and traveled together for Joseph Rosendo's Travelscope for more than fifteen years. Yes, it's wonderful, but it can also be a stress on our

Sharing a *wurst* with my wife and producer Julie on a shoot in Wittenberg, Germany (2015)

relationship. Traveling around a country working 12-hour action-packed, creatively intense days with a crew in tow is pretty exhausting. And, let's just say, we don't always agree. After 12 seasons and a million miles, we have almost figured out how to avoid stepping on each other's toes. And while we are in some of the most romantic locations in the world, we're not on vacation. Nevertheless, every now and then we're able to carve out a moment or two for ourselves. At those times I remember why traveling with the

115

woman I love is a dream come true and one I dearly missed during my early years as a travel writer and broadcaster.

Singles romance — is that an oxymoron? It takes two to tango, I hear.

So many good things come in twos — peaches and cream, wind and rain, turtle doves and love birds. And most people travel in pairs. It's been that way since Noah's Ark — the first "no frills" ocean cruise. Wherever you go you find couples — the more romantic the spot, the greater the congregation of lovers.

It must be some kind of primal instinct. Couples can smell a romantic spot thousands of miles away. They flock to them like a herd of wildebeests to a waterhole. They know how to read brochures. They can spot all the phrases that spell romance with a capital "R": "private jacuzzis," "sugar-white beaches," "classic guitars," "balmy nights," "king-sized beds" and "in-room entertainment."

As a travel journalist it is my job to experience some of the most beautiful, spectacularly romantic places in the world — alone. While in Los Cabos, Mexico it was hard to keep my mind on my note pad when through the open window I could see lovers strolling off to secret hideaways. High season or low season quickly becomes "off" season when you're alone in a romantic destination.

At times my surroundings have been so lovely that I felt like weeping all over my complimentary fruit basket. Once I actually left a hotel at two a.m. because it was too painful to spend another lonely night there.

"Is there anything wrong, sir?" the puzzled night clerk asked.

"The bed's too big," I muttered.

What do you do if you must travel solo?

You could try picking places that aren't romantic. Sounds like a fine idea, except travel itself is so darn romantic. It's the anticipation that something special is about to happen. We all know romance is just waiting for us — lounging around the Piazza San Marco in Venice, basking on Ipanema Beach in Rio or strolling the Champs-Élysées in Paris.

Ah, yes, one could always fall in love. It's more difficult to do than the travel brochures and romantic novels would have us believe, but it does happen. What could be more magical than to be in Europe and in love, in India and in love, in South America and in love — or, well, anywhere and in love.

If not in love with a person, then how about with travel itself? Maybe that's the solution. You can be excited by the unknown, swept away by the freedom and titillated by the exotic.

"A travel adventure has no substitute. It is the ultimate experience, your one big opportunity for flair," said writer Rosalind Massow.

So, the next time you're with your loved one in a romantic spot, cast a sympathetic glance at the solitary

figure walking the beach — it could be someone you
know caught in a fit of romantic longing.

Summertime Blessings

I love traveling through wine country. Yes, my fondness for wine has something to do with it, but it's all about location, location, location. The wine countries of the world are located in some of the world's most scenic spots. The grapes are finicky that way — they demand the very best. I'm blessed to live in California, which has 3,674 wineries and 139 American Vinicultural Areas. One thing wine producers and wine lovers love to do is celebrate. A stay in wine country during one of the many festivals is magical.

"Summertime and the livin' is easy."

It is late on Vintner's Night at the Napa Valley Wine Auction — a yearly extravaganza of wine, food and money well spent. This year's theme is *A Symphony for the Senses* and at tonight's event, hosted by Sterling and Mumm Cuvee Napa wineries, the night is indeed musical, albeit not symphonic.

It's a hot day's cool night and the theme is Greek on the terrace of Sterling Vineyards, perched 300 feet above the valley floor. A costumed quartet that earlier was hammering out Zorba-like tunes while three professional dancers and a dozen Grecian wannabes sashayed across the floor has inexplicably switched to jazz. A guest has commandeered the microphone and is improvising a decent rendition of the Gershwin and Heywood operatic lullaby, *"Summertime."*

"Fish are jumpin' and the cotton is high."

Actually, it is the vines that are six feet high, lush and deep green. The plants are leaf-heavy and hold the promise of fall harvest in their tiny green fruit. There is something about summer in wine country that is unlike any place else. Just the sight of the rows upon rows of *Vitis vinifera* makes me happy and hopeful. I came to drink, taste and learn, but also to be in proximity to the vines and their keepers.

"Your daddy's rich and your mama's good lookin'."

There is a wide diversity of people that populate these hallowed hills, yet a quick look around any of the Wine Auction's official gatherings would produce a demographic survey consistent with the above lyric. To own a patch of this venerable earth takes a larger than ostrich-sized nest egg, and although riches do not necessarily attract beauty, they do not seem to repel it either. That is not to say the beauty I sense is only skin deep. Nurtured by the Valley's natural peace and the serenity that comes with doing what you love, the Valley's gentlemen and lady farmers radiate health, confidence and charm. The parade of robust and smiling countenances and fashionably-attired sinewy physiques keeps me in a state of covetous excitement. It's not that these gracious, elegant-looking folk have no problems — we all have problems — theirs just seem more appealing.

"So hush, little baby, don't you cry."

In the midst of these harmonious and convivial scenes, my mind races back to summertimes past and those with whom I shared them engulfed in love — that height of intoxication that makes all seasons linger, but summer even more so. Summer epitomizes the height of pleasure, and even in wine country where fall brings the year's reward, it is in the summer that the fruit gathers the strength and maturity it needs to produce a fine vintage. My memories of other summers will not fade; they are as vivid as yesterday — those other faces, other songs and other tastes.

On my last day in the Valley, I sit on a bench that overlooks the Oakford Vineyards. Owner Catherine Ball has dubbed the seat her "Blessing Bench."

"What's a blessing?" asks her granddaughter.

"Why do you ask?" her mother replies.

"Because grandma counts hers."

So on my last day, I sit on the blessed bench and I try to take in the sounds and sights of the valley before me — the manicured vines, bees buzzingly at work (Why do we think that bees only work?), puffs of white dandelion fuzz riding a breeze, the song of a robin, a mosaic of tiny wildflowers, the mature oaks that protect the vineyard, a gecko darting under a bush and the distant hum of the highway that will take me back to the city.

Suddenly I hear a woman's laughter. It is followed closely by a man's. I cannot tell their age or race or creed, but there is an intimacy that is unmistakable.

I awaken from my reverie and discover a germ of melancholy. And so, from my hilltop perch under a brilliant cloudless sky, surrounded by nature and man's riches and within earshot of lovers' laughter, I shake my head — and count my blessings.

A Travel Romance Test

If you want to get to know someone intimately, travel with them. Traveling with a partner can be an opportunity to share the best of times. However, take a trip with the wrong person and it can quickly become a disaster. Travel is a great test of character. It's especially helpful when you feel you've found a likely candidate for your significant other. No doubt there are certain things you'd like to know about that person. A trip together will give you some answers.

There's no denying that travel is romantic. Inside our heads dance images of exotic places where new experiences await

To be alive and in love and in Paris —
c'est si bon (2016)

— places where we can imagine ourselves free of the ties that bind, roaming the world in search of adventure.

In my fantasies I am always traveling with someone I love. Travel gives you the opportunity to share something significant and to create memories together. It could be anything and anywhere — sunset in Puerto Vallarta, Michelangelo's David in Florence, a play in London, a dinner on the Côte d'Azur, a colorful cab ride in New York, a secluded beach on Martinique — beautiful times, exciting times, humorous times, peaceful times when you look at each other and share a smile of understanding and appreciation.

I've managed to travel abroad with every woman I've ever been serious about. Some people require their significant other to pass a strict "meet the family" test — but I'd rather see how my partner survives the humidity of Italy in August or the mosquitoes of Lapland, Finland in June.

It's a difficult test because, although travel is romantic and exciting, it can also be a pain. And since time is limited, every experience must be the best — a sure recipe for disappointment and high tension.

Traveling with the one you love is a joy, but you must also master the art of diplomacy. There are constantly important decisions to make, compromises to negotiate and always "miles to go before you sleep."

On a trip you have a chance to see your special someone at their best — and worst. And they have a chance to see you. Are you forgiving of each other's lapses of patience and intelligence? If you find yourself in Spain wishing your companion were in the Amazon (river, that is), you've got a problem.

I'm happy to say all of my companions passed the travel test with flying colors — or at least I thought they did. But perhaps that's part of the romance of travel too. Everything looks better, including your mate, and experiences are painted in broad strokes with brilliant, rosy colors — especially once you've returned home.

Still, here are a few warning signals to help you identify a special friend with whom you are definitely not on the road to romance:

Loved One complains about traffic, bills or headache while en route to the airport.

Loved One claims that citizens of the country visited are "rude," "quaint," "uncivilized," "weird" or, worst of all, "cute."

Loved One is more concerned with the stars on the hotel than the ones in the sky.

Loved One looks at the Eiffel Tower, the pyramids of Giza or the Taj Mahal and says, "Hmm, architecturally interesting."

If any of these occur, travel aficionados have but one alternative: Dump Them. Your unimaginative paramour couldn't feel the romance of travel or see the beauty of the world if it came up and bit them on the nose.

As Ralph Waldo Emerson said, "Though we travel the world over to find the beautiful, we must carry it with us or we will find it not" — that's true for romance, too.

Lifting Your Fork

Get Stuffed — It's a Buffet

When my brother Ron and I would get together we had a menagerie of stories to tell. He was five years younger than me, but we shared many of our family's significant times together. He was there on all those one-day family trips to Key West, through every high school and college sweetheart I won and lost and my biggest fan during my trials and tribulations as an actor. I was his big brother. During my therapy years I once demanded that our relationship change and we have a more equal relationship. He pondered the idea for moment, gave me a look, which was the visual equivalent of "Naww" and said, "I like you're my big brother." And so I always was, his big brother. Nevertheless, he could teach me a thing or two as well. For instance, he was a waiter for many years and had a deep hatred of brunches. The waste troubled him, the quality troubled him, and the lack of tips for delivering water and coffee really ticked him off. Nevertheless, because I was his big brother, he shared with me a few tricks of the trade so that I could make the most of what he considered to be a bad meal.

I hate buffet brunch.

First of all, you have to serve yourself. When I go out I want to be pampered.

 Secondly, I always eat too much. Eating too much at a buffet brunch is easy. What else should you do in a roomful of desserts? It's partly the temptation and partly playing the brunch game. Arrayed before you is more food than you could eat in a lifetime. It's the abundance that thrills — the excess.

Thirdly, buffet brunches are expensive. A good one can range from $40 to $60 per person — for breakfast, no less. I don't know about you, but I can buy a pretty good sit-down dinner for $25.

In general, buffets are convenient for feeding large quantities of people quickly and easily. They're especially useful at bar mitzvahs, wedding receptions and wakes. But when I go out to eat, I don't want to be treated like one of the mob. I want to feel special.

And they're too much work. At some of the more elaborate buffet brunches you need a map and a battle plan to get breakfast. Recently, I heard a restaurant reviewer give his viewers some tips on how to "do" a particular $50 brunch — scout the area first; grab the expensive stuff and don't fill up on salads. Who wants to work that hard on a Sunday morning?

Yet, the <u>real</u> reason I hate buffets is because of the Nordic Horse Smorgasbord.

When I was a kid in Miami, once a week my father would drag us to the Nordic Horse Smorgasbord. It had a huge orange horse straddling the entrance and a 10-foot banner that read, "All-You-Can-Eat — $1.99."

Now, even when I was a kid $1.99 was not a lot of money. Can you imagine the quality of the food? And yet, each week we stuffed ourselves on cold macaroni salads, greasy Swedish meatballs (shaped like a ball, but don't ask about the meat), lumpy mashed potatoes, canned vegetables, tasteless entrees and artificially flavored, colored and prepared puddings.

They had the worst food and the meanest waitresses in Miami. But it was "All-You-Can-Eat — $1.99!"

It's no wonder the waitresses were mean. Do you know what 15% of $1.99 is? And my father always tipped less — "We served ourselves, didn't we?" he'd say.

In fact, although it was "All-You-Can-Eat — $1.99!", once through the buffet line "repeats" on anything had to be ordered from the waitress. And the waitresses were especially nasty if you asked for more. We always did. We had to. My father didn't bring us to the Nordic Horse for a single helping. He was determined to get his money's worth. Although I always asked for seconds, I never went for thirds — I didn't have the guts. Each time we asked for a "repeat" the waitress would scowl as if we were greedy little hogs.

My brother held the record for the most food devoured by a member of my family at the Nordic Horse Smorgasbord. I remember the night. The waitress was picking up the dishes from our second

131

helping and asked the required, "Any more here?" And my brother said, "Repeat, please."

The waitress's left eyebrow arched sharply. "Are you going to eat it all, son?" she asked.

"Repeat, please," replied my brother.

My brother Ronnie Rosendo, age six and already a snappy dresser

My mother was embarrassed. My father grinned, as if to say, "That's my boy!" And I was horrified — I thought the waitress was going to kill him.

For the next hour the battle of wills waged. The waitress would begrudgingly bring the food and my pencil-thin seven-year-old brother would say, "Repeat, please."

She tried everything to stop him.

Praise — "He's a big eater, isn't he?" Wonder — "Where does he put it all?" Fear — "You don't want to get sick." Threat — "Remember, no doggie-bags allowed!"

The whole time my brother just kept saying, "Repeat, please" as cool as a lump of Nordic Horse Smorgasbord gravy.

That night my brother had thirds on salads and meatballs, fourths on chicken and mashed potatoes and fifths on dessert — plus two glasses of chocolate milk.

He was my hero. He had eaten more Nordic Horse food than anyone I knew, and had survived to tell the tale.

That was a long time ago. My brother's gone now, but I think of him often. He was my friend, my fan and my witness. I think about us as kids — about the bad times, the good times and about the time he made the waitress at the Nordic Horse Smorgasbord choke on her tapioca pudding.

The Invisible Man

When we were kids my younger brother Ron always wanted to hang out with me. Being a good big brother, I'd devise interesting ways he could do that. One was to be my waiter. He'd put up our TV tables in the living room and with a dishtowel draped over his arm he'd go through an elaborate process of telling me what was on the menu, taking my order and serving me whatever my mother had prepared for dinner that night. My mother would yell at me from the kitchen to "stop torturing your brother and get your own dinner," but my brother loved the game as much as I did. Years later, when we were living together in Los Angeles, I brilliantly recalled those good old days and got him a job as a waiter at a local French restaurant. It was the first of many positions he had as a waiter, sommelier and maître 'd. It was a stroke of genius on my part. He was a natural and I've never had better service.

Do you remember the movie, *The Invisible Man?* Here's a synopsis: *Handsome, altruistic doctor makes a discovery which he dreams will save the world, but which transforms him into a crazed, schizophrenic nowhere man. Hunted and alone, he rages through London murdering his*

*enemies, until finally, fatally wounded, he lies dying. As the
credits roll and he gradually fills in, his life slowly fades out.*

The original may have expired, but playing
citywide and waiting to take your orders are: "The
Invisible Men."

 I encountered one of
them on a recent Saturday
night, when my compan-
ion and I stopped into
Bravo, a cafe/restaurant on
the Third Street Promen-
ade in Santa Monica, for an after-theater snack. "Could
we just have coffee and dessert?" I asked the hostess.

"Certainly," she said, "Follow me."

At our table a pleasant looking young waiter
arrived and asked, "What would you like?"

"A cheesecake to share," I replied.

Without warning, a hideous transformation akin to
Lon Chaney, Jr. as Larry Talbot becoming the wolfman
took place. After a pause, he grimaced horribly, let out a
soul-wrenching sigh, rolled his eyes and glared
murderously at the hostess.

It was obvious he had disapproved of our order
— in his opinion, it was too meager for a Saturday
night — yet, in his mind, his expressions of disgust
were not visible to us.

"That's fine," he said, grinning like a lunatic (his
teeth were clenched, but his face was smiling), "And
to drink?"

"Two cappuccinos," I said, which started him off on another round of grimaces, sighs and eye rolls.

After he left, I turned to my friend. "He wasn't very pleased with our order, was he?"

"No," she said, "And he must either think we're blind or that he's invisible."

"Well, I've seen the movie, and there's only one defense against the Invisible Man — make yourself invisible, too." We rose to leave.

"What's the problem?" asked the hostess.

"It was frightening," I said, "Our waiter thinks he's the Invisible Man."

"Would you like another waiter?"

"No, just another restaurant."

What is it that makes some service people think that the public is too dumb to notice their *at-ti-tude?* Is it because many of us are too polite to respond to the obvious offense? Perhaps we're intimidated by the prospect of causing a ruckus. Perhaps we're afraid that the romantic *tête-à-tête* we planned will deteriorate into a heated *mano a mano* with the waiter.

So we put up with the chilly treatment. We settle for less. And the rumor spreads that they are invisible, and no matter how much they huff and puff and harrumph, we won't even notice.

But in truth, the secret potion doesn't work: we see them, we hear them, and although we may sympathize (yes, it's hard to serve the public), we know what SERVICE means and how to ask for it.

Joseph Rosendo

My advice to the new crop of Invisible Men is to take a warning from the original: first you're invisible, and then you — disappear.

Smile — You're the Entertainment

Some people are allergic to clowns; I'm adverse to mimes. I think it's a holdover from a career of acting classes where sooner or later you are asked to pretend you have something that you don't or that you're doing something that you're not. I'd never do it, but, I must admit, Woody Allen punching out a particularly insistent mime in Paul Mazursky's "Scenes From A Mall" gave me an evil, vicarious thrill.

You go to a restaurant for brunch. It's Sunday morning, you've had a long hard week and you want to relax before you start another long hard week. You sit down, order, then you spot him. He's cruising the restaurant, eyeing every diner. He's dressed all in black and his face is white — clown white.

You look away, but it's too late. He's spotted you, and he's heading your way. There's no place to hide. You try to ignore him, but there's no avoiding him. He's *The Mime*, and he's here to entertain you. You have just become another victim of "live entertainment."

Don't get me wrong. I like to be entertained. I love the circus, I love music and I'm a big fan of Marcel Marceau. But I like to decide where and when

I want to be an audience. And if I'm going to be a part of someone's act, I want to know my lines.

In a restaurant I want to eat, drink and create my own merriment. I'm there for the food and the ambience. If I wanted to see a show I'd be at the theater. If I wanted to feel uncomfortable I'd visit my ex-wife.

It's really not the performer's fault. He's just doing his job. Some of them could use a little sensitivity choosing likely victims, though. Like the mime that rubbed his stomach and eyed the plate of the woman at the table next to me for a solid ten minutes — long after her smile grew thin.

Actually, most of them are great at picking their "audience." They just chose me. And I'm a professional crowd. Before I became a travel writer I was an actor, so I empathize with the performer to the extent that I always feel obligated to be a responsive audience. I applaud for the musician at the piano bar, ooh and ahh for the chain saw juggler and request a song from the roving mariachis.

So maybe it shows. Or maybe I just exude some kind of musk performers sense that says, "I really want a balloon shaped like a giraffe" or "I'm a sucker for sappy songs."

But enough is enough. I'm tired of being accosted in the middle of my Eggs Benedict. Arise fellow diners — cast off your chains of discomfiture and refuse the animal balloons, ignore the mime's pratfall, let the magician use his own coat to put out his cigarette and tell Los Strolling Guitars that you never want to hear "La Bamba" again.

But alas, although I may incite you to rebel, don't expect me to join the revolution. I just can't get myself to say, "Get Lost" to anyone who would pin a paper heart to their chest.

Meatless Fridays

When I was born my father put a ten-inch baseball bat in the crib with me. Since his poverty and father kept him from his dream of playing major league baseball, I was supposed to live his dream for him. I was good, but not that good, so at the age of 14 I hung up my cleats and

Joey as a scrappy nine-year-old Miami Little League second baseman (1955)

gave away my baseball mitt. Until then, I ate, slept, talked, breathed and dreamed baseball. While other kids had their movie heroes, mine did their super deeds on a baseball diamond. They were all New York Yankees and at the top of the list was Mickey Mantle. Whenever I needed to escape the hubbub that was a part of living with my parents, I didn't need an imaginary friend. I had Mickey Mantle.

Mickey Mantle's dead. This may not be news to you, but I'm still getting over it. He was my hero.

Oh, I know he practically drank himself to death and squandered his youth and talents in bars, but he was still one of the best ballplayers. In a game glutted with stars, he shines still.

He hit 536 regular season and 18 World Series (still a record) home runs. He was the American League's Most Valuable Player three times, won the Triple Crown in 1956 and once launched a ball so far that it came within a few feet of leaving the old Yankee Stadium all together. Of all the old Bronx Bombers, he was the most explosive.

Ever since I can remember, the Yankees were my team and Mickey Mantle was my super hero.

I adopted the Yankees early in life. I was a child in Miami when I looked at the sports page and found the

New York Yankees planted at the top of the American League standings — a mere 23 games ahead of the pack.

"That's my team!" I said. Hey, if you've got a choice, why not pick the best?

In the 1950s Mickey Mantle was the Yankee star and my idol. I even snagged his autograph when the team played an exhibition game in Miami the summer I was ten. It was my prized possession, and when my mother threw it away "by accident" years later, I was heartbroken. Well, I guess she didn't know that Mickey Mantle was not only the sports icon of my youth, but one of the finest dinner companions I've ever had.

My father was Roman Catholic. And although he didn't follow all the rules, "Meatless Friday" was a papal edict he adhered to religiously. Every Friday from the time I could sit in a high chair, my family went to *Mendez* for fish.

Café Mendez Restaurant and Bar was housed in an old two-story building on Flagler Street in downtown Miami. To reach the dining rooms you walked up six concrete steps, through a screen door and into a large room. That room was partitioned into four smaller rooms by plywood walls that didn't quite reach the ceiling and were painted an unappetizing green. Checkered black and white linoleum covered the floor.

We always ate in the front section that overlooked the street. The wooden tables were draped in bleached, starched and ironed white tablecloths and from the kitchen downstairs wonderful smells wafted up to us. The room held three tables, and now and then someone peered around the partition and contemplated joining us in the room, but my father always dissuaded them with his patented version of the evil eye.

The restrooms were down a narrow hallway. Halfway down the hall, a small green door led down to the bar at street level. I often faked going to the restroom for a chance to peek in at the denizens dwelling below.

The scene downstairs was a world apart from the

sedate family-friendly atmosphere upstairs. Here the floor was colorfully tiled and the ceiling, walls and lights were a brilliant white. Seated at tables with plates of *arroz con pollo* or *puerco asado* in front of them, Cuban men, in groups, spoke at the speed of light and punctuated their verbal exclamations with glasses that sloshed red wine onto the pink marble table tops. Others smoked fat, dark, oily *cigarros*, drank dirt-black *café Cubano* and listened skeptically, waiting impatiently for a chance to butt in.

Each time I ventured into this domain I felt excited — something not quite safe, but spirited was happening here. Whenever the waiter spotted me he'd shoo me upstairs. His look seemed to say, "This is no place for children."

Rodriquez was our waiter. If he was not working, we dined elsewhere. Although my father was not a big tipper, he was still a stickler about service. He wanted non-stop bread in the basket, coffee in his cup and water in his glass. Rodriquez satisfied his desires.

So, every Friday we'd arrive at *Mendez*, enter our private dining room, sit at our assigned places and order the same one-plate dinner: A breaded and deep fried red snapper, French fries and a small salad (a piece of lettuce with a slice of tomato on top). There were cruets of oil and vinegar for dressing, homemade Cuban bread, water for my brother and me, coffee for my father and iced tea for my mother. If the mood struck them, my parents might order dessert — a *flan* or a bowl of *arroz con leche*.

I'm not sure when Mickey Mantle started joining me for dinner. I must have been eight because my brother was still in the high chair. I remember my parents were discussing their issue-of-the-day — something she bought which she shouldn't or someplace he stayed longer than he should — in any case, in the middle of their squabble, the lights in the room seemed to dim and in strolled The Mick as big as life.

"Hi kid, what's for dinner," he said, giving me a wink.

I realized he was talking to me.

"Fish and French fries, as always, Mr. Mantle," I replied.

"Sounds tasty," he said grabbing a chair at another table. "Come over and join me."

"Okay, Mr. Mantle," I said, getting up.

"Call me Mickey," he answered grinning.

My father broke the spell.

"Joey, where are you going?"

"Uh, nowhere. I was, uh, just stretching," I said, stretching.

"Sit down, and finish eating."

"Right," I stammered, sitting down.

"If you don't hurry up, you'll be the last to finish."

"Sure," I said, as the restaurant light began to brighten again.

"Shhh!" said my mother pointing to the partition, which separated the rooms, "Don't yell. The people in the other room will hear you."

"Don't shush me," my father growled, "I pay for my dinner. Don't shush me."

"Just don't talk so loud, you'll bother other people."

"Let them hear if they want," he said raising his voice. "I never bother anyone."

"Ah," I thought, "The next issue-of-the-day has been selected."

As their new quarrel began, the lights dimmed and Mickey was gesturing to me to stay put.

"Don't worry, kid, I'll come over there," he said, pulling up his chair and joining me at my special spot at the end of the table.

"How do you like the fish, Mick," I said. He didn't need to order, he could share mine.

"Fine, kid, just fine," he said in his Oklahoma drawl. "This is a fine restaurant."

"Well, I like it because they cook the fish just right and you notice that the French fries are crispy on the outside, but tender inside."

"And that there's a fresh piece of lettuce," he added waving the lettuce leaf in the air.

Mick and I had a grand old time that night and many more Fridays afterwards. While my parents argued, we discussed hitting, running, the Yankee's chance for another world championship and the fine food at *Café Mendez*.

"When will I see you again, Mickey?" I asked as my father was paying the bill.

"How about next Friday night," he answered,

rising and brushing the Cuban bread crumbs off his shirt, "Same restaurant, okay?"

"Same time, same place," I said.

"And if you're ever in New York — look me up," he said, heading for the door and fading away.

"I will," I said, "I will."

By the time the U. S. Conference of Catholic Bishops lifted the Meatless Friday dictum, I had stopped eating with my parents, *Mendez* was razed as part of a Miami urban renewal project and I had forgotten about my dinners with Mickey.

Yet, years later when I happened to be in New York and discovered that the Yankees "Old Timers Day" game was scheduled — "I looked him up."

It was a perfect day. During his one time at bat in the three-inning exhibition game Mickey got a base hit and drove in a run. And later that night, in the regularly scheduled game, the Yankees beat the Baltimore Orioles when Reggie Jackson hit a home run in the bottom of the ninth inning.

After the game, I waited at the players' entrance. Perhaps I'd get another chance at that autograph. Perhaps I'd just say hello. Although I saw Roger Maris and Billy Martin, *The Mick* had left earlier.

Yes, I was sad when Mickey Mantle passed away. He meant a lot to me. I think I fell in love with dining out and restaurants because of my dinners with

Mickey. I'm sorry I never got to meet him again. I'm sorry I never got to thank him for baseball fans everywhere — and for that little kid who dined with him at *Café Mendez*.

Travel Power

The Walls Came Tumbling Down
Travel Addict

The Walls Came Tumbling Down

*"Travel is fatal to prejudice, bigotry and narrow-mindedness,"
wrote Mark Twain in his delightful travel book, "The
Innocents Abroad." It's a quote that I've used to close every
show since the days when Travelscope was a radio show on
KIEV/KRLA in Los Angeles. From 1985 to 2008 I did close to
1,100 broadcasts and my show's "audio-documentary" style
evolved into Joseph Rosendo's Travelscope on PBS. I love
Twain's quote because it's true, direct and provocative. At a
time when a U.S. president can talk about "shithole countries"
and display a lack of empathy, respect and decency without
repercussions, Mark Twain's words stand as a testament to*

Tea with a holy man
in Orchha, Madhya
Pradesh, India. He
had just gifted us
with a blessing cere-
mony in the temple
behind us. (2009)

our common humanity. Twain's quote goes on to champion travel as a national necessity, "…many of our people need it sorely on these accounts. Broad, wholesome, charitable views of men and things cannot be acquired by vegetating in one little corner of the earth all one's lifetime." Twain understood the power of travel to change us and through us, the world.

I love travel because it changes you, whether it's an international journey or a weekend getaway. Travel changes both your perspective on life and your priorities. Travel forces us to see our place in comparison to other places, our lives in comparison to other lives.

I remember when I went to Europe in 1969; it was my first trip abroad. I was traveling with an acting troupe from UCLA, performing for the US troops based in Germany. Europe could never be like that again. My whole world changed. I never knew how much I was missing, what a small part of the world I lived in. Every sensation was so intense.

The first night a few of us "honorary lieutenants" went to dinner at the officers' club. The waiter asked if we would like some wine. Yes, we said and he brought over a bottle for us to try. I was nominated as the wine taster. (Hey, I was living in California now. I had tasted wine.) I waited patiently while he opened the bottle, handed me the cork and poured a bit of the liquid into my glass.

Although I was not yet sure why people did it, I'd been to the movies so I knew the proper procedure for tasting wine. I carefully perused the liquor for color, swirled the wine around the glass to check out its legs, stuck my nose in the glass and breathed in its bouquet.

Then I raised the glass to sip a bit. Yet when the golden nectar touched my lips, I swallowed the offering in a gulp.

"You're not supposed to swill it, Joey," my friends laughed. "Just taste it."

I looked at the waiter, my taste buds aglow. "Whatever that is bring me more!" I said. I had never tasted anything like it. It was new — delicious — sweet and intoxicating — and became a metaphor for my first travel experience. The quality and the promises it offered stunned me.

This was a world I knew nothing about. "How long has this been going on?" I wondered. I was seduced by the honeyed taste of knowledge. Perhaps it wasn't an apple at all, but a good *1964 Piesporter Auslese*  that Eve sampled in the Garden of Eden. No wonder she risked God's wrath to take a bite. This was travel at its best: an inner discovery that life could be different. My first European trip revealed possibilities — both external and internal — that I had never imagined.

Each time I travel I try to make new discoveries. I hope to find endless variety in the way people live their lives, and take home infinite options for my own life. It's a relief to realize that my way of life is not the only way — what a burden to think that it is!

When I became a travel writer, it was because I

loved to travel and because I was idealistic enough to want to change the world. Child of the '60s that I am, I felt that if people could meet each other they would see that we are much more alike than different.

While politicians harp on our differences, good travelers are sensitive to our similarities. In Peru, a Quechua Indian, a modern-day descendant of the Incas, told me, "We know you are part of our world. It is the politicians that divide us, but the people, we are the same."

Of course, as my travel writing and broadcasting career progressed, it became clear that making a living at travel was not all a bed of roses. But then I would get a note from a listener thanking me for a radio show or a reader who appreciated a story. My beliefs held firm.

And then on November 9, 1989 the Berlin Wall came tumbling down. Now I'm sure my colleagues who do political talk radio shows could tell us why

The Berlin Wall's East Side Gallery, an instrument of oppression transformed into a canvas of creation (2014)

the wall collapsed. Economic mismanagement. Political corruption. An unworkable system. A desire for the free marketplace. Good solid reasons.

But here's another for you — travel. It was the East Germans' obsession with the freedom to travel that tore holes in the Wall. While thousands fled for a new life, hundreds of thousands more just wanted the freedom to take a peek — to sightsee.

Witness the masses that strolled through the great gapes in the Wall for a weekend in West Berlin. They acted like tourists! Amazed with the differences and touched by the similarities, they looked around, bought a few necessities and loaded up on souvenirs.

So maybe I'm not too far off. Maybe travel can change the world. Maybe travel can bring peace. Maybe meeting each other will keep us from killing each other. The Berlin Wall today — tomorrow the world!

Travel Addict

My first real travel experience was when I joined my friend Bill Trammel and his family on their road trip to Ohio. We drove through Georgia, the Carolinas, Virginia and West Virginia. They got a kick out of my excitement at seeing a hill in Orlando; South Florida doesn't have many of them. Imagine my thrill and their chuckles when I saw the

Having a smoke with the Huli Wigman of Papua New Guinea
(2008)

Appalachians. That trip was the start of my "travel habit." I was hooked and from then on I'm always looking for my next adventure.

The travel brochures talk about creating memories that will live forever — "a once-in-a-lifetime moment that you'll never forget," they boast.

Kodak has made many fortunes convincing us that we can freeze the moments forever on little pieces of photographic paper. And as memory-joggers, they do a pretty good job.

But even as we snap the picture we know it pales in comparison to the real thing. We can't capture a memory or freeze the moment.

The travel experience is like an addiction — the more you travel, the more you crave it. It can be a powerful drug. The late Edward Abbey wrote of some tourists who, mesmerized by the desert landscape of Utah, wandered off into the beauty of the wilderness with no water, food or gear. Their bodies were never found.

Handled well, travel is an addiction that can be managed and certainly enjoyed. Short weekend trips can keep the urge at bay for a while. A week or two of a summer vacation can take the edge off. But true travel addicts live with a constant yearning to be on the road that can only be alleviated by a major expedition, an adventure, a grand escape to a different world — or at least a different part of the world.

It is a habit that needs to be constantly fed, an

experience that needs to be constantly renewed. That's because peak experiences are difficult to repeat, recall or relive — that's the underlying tragedy of human existence.

If you travel merely to complete an international checklist of "points-of-interest," then you'll probably be satisfied with your snapshots of the Eiffel Tower. But if you travel to expand yourself and to learn about new worlds and new peoples, then you're a real travel addict — and you need to take a hit as often as your budget will allow.

Yet no matter what travel experiences I look back on, my pleasant memories often become shrouded in forgetfulness. It's almost impossible for me to truly recall the brilliance of the hot sun on a rice paddy in Indonesia, the mysterious smile in the eyes of a Nepalese woman in a marketplace in Kathmandu or the profound silence of a starlit night at Machu Picchu. No matter how good my memory is or how evocative my photos are, I have forgotten. I am forgetting now ... .

But I take heart. A travel addiction can always be treated, if not cured. The remedy? Take another trip ... and another ... and another ... ."

Road Bumps

What I Learned on the Radio
I Am Sam, Too
A Cultural Cryptogram
Europe Remembered
The Fear of Travel

What I Learned on the Radio

I did Travelscope, my travel radio show, on two conservative talk radio stations, KIEV and KNRY in Los Angeles, for twenty-three and a half years. My show gave me the outlet for my travel adventures, was my magic carpet ride to amazing people of every race, creed and nationality and allowed me to share my philosophy of life. It was invaluable training in preparation for my PBS television series and allowed my dream of traveling the world to come true. The downside was being in an environment saturated with anger, negativity and hatred. Although my liberal ideals and I were safety quarantined in my glass studio, from time to time the animosity filling the hallways and airways seeped in under the door spoiling all it touched, including me.

"Travel is fatal to prejudice, bigotry and narrow-mindedness"

Mark Twain

In the course of a broadcast day there are people who call talk radio stations who are awash with hatred.

I envision them out there sitting in darkened rooms, surrounded by the clutter of their lives. I can see them barricaded from the outside world in a cubicle filled with dust and cobwebs. It's a room where no light enters. The static from their radio is their only company. They sit and wait for their chance to "Talk Back." Within these rooms, they concoct their diatribes of loathing. Within these cramped and lifeless spaces, they form their scorching words and destructive thoughts — in these dark, dank and dirty places.

Yet, these are not real rooms at all, but the compartments of their minds. It's in their own minds that they construct their monuments to hatred. In their hearts they nurture the seeds of hate originally planted in a distant past by a seemingly loving hand with imagined slights and injustices and give the budding weeds food and space to grow. Soon the hate invades all of the nooks and crannies of their existence. It becomes all that they live for — it becomes who they are.

I have produced Travelscope Radio for more than two decades and normally these people do not call my radio show. I hope it's because of the atmosphere I create, but it probably is because travel is too inclusive, too hopeful, too life affirming to attract these hate mongers. Still, I hear them on other shows.

There are shows on the airways that elicit and, in fact, encourage callers who harbor the kind of racial, religious and cultural hatred that I am speaking about.

Often times the hosts do not even believe in the positions they espouse on the air; as one once told me, "Hate makes good radio."

"A good holiday is one spent among people whose notions of time are vaguer than yours."
J.B. Priestly

Although I am rarely subjected to such poison, I recently received one such phone call. Not on the air, the caller was too cowardly to call the show. Hopefully she knew that she would not be allowed to spew forth her venom, that I would hang up on her or that my engineer, who I had instructed accordingly, would bleep out her comments. She called my office and left a message.

I was in Mexico doing a live remote broadcast from the Presidente Inter-Continental Hotel Los Cabos. I love Mexico and the Mexican people. There are few more beautiful and naturally rich countries. There are few more welcoming and generous people. Perhaps, she sensed my enthusiasm for the culture and the country and it flicked the red switch on in her explosive mind. Whatever the reason she ranted and raved for several minutes about how all Mexicans were illegal aliens, against Spanish being allowed in the schools, the hordes of Chicano gangs in the streets and the general ruination of the United States caused by Mexicans.

I didn't listen to the entire message, because no matter how much I protect myself, I know hatred is as infective and deadly as any killer virus. The main thrust of her diatribe was that I shouldn't be talking about Mexico at all because no true American would ever want to go to Mexico. Finally she ran out of steam and hung up. She soon called back and left another message along the same line, except this time, interestingly enough, she left her name and number.

No, I didn't call her back. Perhaps, I should have. Perhaps, it was a cry for help. But I've learned that it does no good to speak to people whose minds are shut so tight. "You can't teach a pig to fly," a friend once told me, "It angers the pig and frustrates the teacher." Yet, in some way I wanted to respond.

I would have said, "Why are you so angry? Who has injured you? What created the holes in your heart that you have filled with hate? Do you not know that hate is more lethal to you than the 357 Magnum in the hand of the gang member that you fear? Do you not know that hate worms its way into the tiniest recesses of our souls and is not easily extracted?

And on that germ of hate other viruses grow and develop into cancers and tumors, and sickness? Is your precious life worth wasting on hating? And, after all, who is it that you really hate? Yourself?

"The wise man travels to discover himself."
James Russell Lowell

I understand this hatred. As a second generation American of Cuban ancestry, I'm not usually the target of the racial and cultural hatred and abuse that caller exhibited towards Mexicans. Most people don't even know what Cubans are or what they are supposed to be like or why they should hate them. If they think of Cubans at all they probably think of Desi Arnaz and Andy Garcia, and now, little Elian Gonzalez. They may think of Fidel Castro, but he's not really Cuban — he's a communist. And everybody hates communists.

When I grew up in Miami there wasn't a Castro to hate. There weren't as many Cubans in Miami as there are today, they weren't in positions of power, and they didn't speak and dream about returning home. Miami was our home. And although people still didn't know who or what Cubans were — they just didn't like them. Even my family didn't like Cubans.

When Castro and the Cuban revolution rode into Havana on January 8, 1959 and thousands of Cubans who supported the dictator Batista had to flee the country and come to Miami, my relatives despised those Cuban refugees. Innocently I asked, "But aren't we Cubans?" "We're not those kinds of Cubans," they told me. "We're Americans. We're Spanish descendants." Well, I didn't even know where Spain was. And we never ate tapas or played futbol. Yellow rice and chicken was our Sunday meal and baseball, not bullfighting, our favorite sport. My relatives' Cuban-hatred confused me.

I was 23 years old and living in Los Angeles

before I admitted I was Cuban. When I was a kid, being Cuban in Miami was not the thing to be. For years, I passed as an Italian. A classmate once asked me what I was and I said, "Half Cuban, half Italian." "Alright," he answered, "We'll kill the Cuban part and let the Italian part live." With a name like Rosendo, pretending to be Italian was natural; after all my uncle Cheo was part Italian. Once or twice not speaking the language almost blew my cover, but fortunately Cubans are also loud, excitable and use their hands profusely when they speak. So Italian was a mask I was able to wear with some semblance of reality.

So yes, I know what it's like to hate yourself. And I can see that self-hatred is the real cause of hatred of others. And yes, I can feel empathy for my caller. I can understand her fears. And I have some good advice for her. Get out, get help, get an airline ticket — and please, don't call back.

I Am Sam, Too

I had a brilliant therapist/friend for more than twenty years. My girlfriend and I started conjoint therapy with Murray Ireland when I was thirty-two. After that relationship broke up in therapy I went by myself for a couple of years. Then I went to Murray with my first wife and when that marriage broke up I went by myself again until I went with my second wife. I was, as they say, "lookin' for love in all the wrong places," but at least I was lookin'. Murray was the perfect love doctor because he was an expert at it. He had a forty-two-year-long marriage with his wife, Sharon, until death did them part. He loved me enough to do nothing short of save my life. Much of what I

am today I owe to Murray. Even though he was as white as snow, he used to say that he would have made a great black preacher. This brother certainly healed my soul.

My friend and teacher Murray Ireland on his boat in Lake Havasu, Arizona

171

Recently I've had some of my travel writer friends pass away. As you get older, so do your friends, colleagues and acquaintances and, then, when you least expect it they disappear — or, at the very least, become invisible.

At several memorials I attended they ask for the attendees to say a word or two about the deceased. Perhaps, to recollect a time spent together, an incident that might shine light on the dearly departed's life and the impact they had on the people they knew.

Waiting to say something, I thought about a minister I once heard speak — or was he a combination of all the ministers I had ever heard speak ... or perhaps I never heard him speak at all ... .

"Brothers and sisters, today I want to speak with you about love," the Reverend said.

The congregation hardly looked up. Love wasn't new. Most of the congregation had sung *Jesus Loves Me* since kindergarten.

"I know Love is not a new topic," the Reverend said, reading their minds. "No, sir. It's not a new topic at all. It's as old as the Bible. It's as old as Methuselah. Older still. It's as old as Adam and Eve."

"No!" he shouted, rousting the congregation from its stupor, "Hell, no, it's as old as heaven and the earth itself."

The congregation rustled. They whispered. The dynamic duo of Hell and Fire they understood, but Hell and Love? This was something different.

"That's how old it is, brethren," the Reverend

continued. "It's young too. It's as young as the baby being born this minute. It's as young as the lovers making love in their car in the church parking lot this instant."

Not a few fathers glanced quickly around to make sure their daughters were within arm's distance. Those who couldn't see them sprouted a row of worry lines across their brows.

"And it's as young as the thoughts and the feelings shooting through your hearts and minds this instant. That's how young love is," he said building steam.

"You don't have to be a genius, you don't have to be a Harvard professor, and you don't have to be a rocket scientist to want it, need it or find it. All you have to do is believe that it exists."

He paused. Although you could hear the birds and the wind in the trees outside, there wasn't a sound in the sanctuary. They waited.

"I don't go to the movies much," he finally said. "I'm afraid of the dark."

A nervous chuckle filled the sanctuary.

"I'm afraid of all that nothingness. I hate sitting alone in a dark theater by myself. Yet, once I hear the others in there moving around with their popcorn, peanuts and other things, I feel better. Although I may be there alone, I don't feel alone. I know that if something happens, I'm going to have company."

The congregation released their tension by laughing out loud.

"So I went to the movies," he said, stepping out from behind the pulpit and down the two short steps to the congregation's level, "I saw a movie entitled, *I Am Sam*."

"It had that bad boy in it," he was reaching for the name, "What's his name. You know, Madonna's husband."

"Joseph of Nazareth?" a little boy offered. Several uncontrollable giggles broke out and the Reverend grinned from ear to ear.

"Thank you, son," he smiled, "But not that Madonna, the other one, the one that was married to Sean Penn."

"Yeah, Sean Penn was in the movie," he said as he grinned and wagged his index finger. "I expected anything. I expected fighting and shooting and cursing and spitting and fornicating. I expected everything, but to my surprise all I found was love."

"You see," he said beginning to stroll up and down the church aisle, "The movie is about an intellectually disabled man, Sam, who is left with a child. His child, mind you. It's not clear how he had this child fall into his lap — something about a homeless woman just wanting a place to stay — but it isn't discussed, because it isn't important."

"What's important is that he loves this child. And because Sam is disabled, the state wishes to take his child away from him."

"Tsk, Tsk," clucked the congregation, although half of them were thinking, "That's a good idea."

"The movie is also about a sharp-witted lawyer who has everything, but love. That's the point, you see. The lawyer has everything, but love and Sam has nothing, but love. Now, brothers and sisters, who do you think is richer? Who would you rather be?"

He didn't give them time to answer, but just rolled right along. "Well, I'll tell you who I'd rather be. I'd rather be simple. Do you know why, brethren? That's because if you have love you have everything. If you don't have love you're poorer than a church mouse — even that raggedy-ass rodent has God."

There was an audible gasp. They had never heard the Reverend curse before and they weren't sure whether they approved. The Reverend never missed a beat.

"Does it shock you," he asked, as he stepped up behind the pulpit again. "Does it shock you that love is the answer? I bet it does. I bet you thought God was the answer. Well, you silly S.O.B.s — God *is* Love.

"Sam doesn't need brains to know that. He knows it instinctively. In fact, if he were any smarter he would be creating a ton of smoke screens to keep love away. Because if you commit to love you have to commit 100% — in order to really have it in all its purity you have to have committed completely — otherwise you won't get it.

"And if you do commit 100% and things go bad you are going to suffer. What could go wrong? Well, your love may die for one. And then where are you? If you haven't protected your little heart against all that hurt — it is going to hurt very, very bad. If you are unwilling to take the very low-lows then brother stay out of the love game. Because the prices you pay for really loving and loving well, can be brutal. Job-like.

"But unlike Job, this is God's reward," the Reverend shouted.

"Thank God," the congregation sighed.

"All that pain and suffering is your just reward for all that loving," whispered the Reverend.

"So what can you do? You can take the easy way out. You can be cold, indifferent. You can close your heart to the person you love. That will ease the pain. But when you close your heart to the person you love, you close your heart to love. Don't let it happen brothers and sisters, don't let it happen. Don't let anyone make you take the easy way out. The road to perdition is an easy road to take. It's a road of protecting yourself from pain and protecting yourself from love. It's not caring. It's badmouthing the person who hurt you. It makes it easy for you in one way, but it kills you in the other.

"Don't take the easy way out. Because if you take the easy way out now, it will be all the harder later. It is fraught with fear, stress, anxiety, depression and unhappiness. Don't give up your loving soul. Don't give up your loving heart. Don't let those who have shut their heart cause you to shut yours.

"I know it hurts. I know you can be hurt. I know those people can be hurtful. But don't give them the satisfaction of turning you from your course on the road to love — because as sure as I stand before you today, as sure as Jesus died on the cross, as sure as Moses led the Israelites to the Promised Land, as sure as Muhammad ascended into the heavens and Buddha reached Nirvana — love is the answer. It is what they were all turning to. Do not turn away from love — face the dark. I'm afraid of that dark more than anything. It's a cold, damp, ugly place where nothing beautiful grows. It's a barren place devoid of warmth and life. It's a small, cramped, tight and airless place. You can't breathe right. You can't sing."

"Hallelujah" the congregation said.

"You can't dance. You can't laugh and you can't cry. You can't feel anything.

"Don't let them convince you to take the easy way out. That way death lies. 'I have set before you life and Death ... therefore chose life,' said Moses to the Israelites before they reached the Promised Land.

"I do the same to you tonight. I put before you love and hate, brotherhood and animosity, self-preservation and the salvation of others. Choose life. Choose love.

"Don't let them turn you away from your mission. Your goal to fulfill your potential — to find love. It's the only thing that is important. The rest is all intellectual bullshit. It's you bullshitting yourself. Thinking that that's what's important — when all it is, is love.

"If you do it, if you hang on to your mission — if you fight the temptation to take the easy way out. You can say, I Am Sam, too."

177

There was a hush on the congregation. The Reverend smiled at all of them and then walked off the pulpit. He walked onto the floor of the little church and hugged the first person he saw — an elderly widow all swathed in black who didn't really know what to make of it. He didn't care. He didn't care what she made of it, what her reality of what was happening was. He just cared that he was doing what he had to do — that he was being true to his mission.

Maybe later there would be repercussions from his actions and his words. But he didn't care. Because he felt safe. He didn't have money. He didn't have status. He didn't have a new car or a big home — he only had love. And that was all he needed to feel safe.

His love for man was enough for him. That was enough for him to feel strong and capable of going through another day. He felt like Sam too.

A Cultural Cryptogram

In my travels I've visited many countries where Buddhism is its peoples' main religious belief. Of the steps on Buddha's eight-fold path to enlightenment the most significant one to me is mindfulness. I've always believed that Right Mindfulness meant to be aware and attentive to our actions and words. Words have as much power as

Receiving the monks' blessings at Cambodia's
Oudong Temple Complex (2017)

actions. Since childhood we are taught to think before we speak for once something is out of our mouths there is no bringing it back. You can say you're sorry, didn't mean it or were misunderstood, but the words are there like atoms bouncing around the universe careening into everyone's hearts and minds, including our own.

I'm crazy. They say I'm crazy. Why? Because I am at a travel press event at an exclusive Los Angeles hotel and I have discovered madness. At the end of this wonderful evening of food, drink and scintillating company — the best of the best — I have sat down in the reasonably sane environment of an elegant lounge and have just heard a nutty idea that has — well, driven me crazy.

I've met (as you always do) people who have enlightened me to the truth that they must live with every day. I've met another writer, a man of intelligence and wit, who has shared with me his strategy and tactic for living life and avoiding pain.

Or was it ignoring pain?

You see he belongs to a particular religious and cultural group who is often the target of derogatory names and jokes. In order to protect himself from these names and the pain they cause him and his friends (who also are members of this religious and cultural group) they address each other by the same derogatory terms that racists and bigots use. Why? "Because by doing so we remove the negative power of those words."

He tells me that he and his friends call each other the k-word, the j-word and the h-word and that it is all right. The philosophy behind this eccentric behavior is that if you belong to a particular ethnic, religious or racial group it's all right to use these fighting words in order to cast off the oppression of the words.

As an example of the truth and success of this tactic, he points out that members of another famously oppressed racial group use the n-word among themselves for the same reasons and to the same effect. The idea being that if you are an "n-word" or a "k-word" it's all right to refer to each other as "n-words" and "k-words."

This is the worst thing I have ever heard.

No, it's not a new concept to me, but every time I hear it I still think it's the worst thing I've ever heard. I tell him that no matter how or when or to whom you say the "n-word," the "k-word" or, in my case, the "s-word," nothing that you can do ever takes away the negative power of those words. No matter how hard you try to pretend that those words are not negative, they can't be anything but negative. That's why they are so powerful. Using these words with each other is like giving yourself a bloody nose before the schoolyard bully does.

No sooner do I say this, than the power of the words become evident. (Obviously, we didn't use hyphenations in conversation, I'm using them here to control the power those words have in print).

"Could you lower your voices," asks one of our

lounge companions. Although we have not raised our voices since we came in, the words have sliced through the buzz that saturates the room, the live piano music and the clinking and tinkling of glasses and plates to cut deeply into our neighbor's peace and tranquility.

With newly lowered voices our debate continues. The fellow reiterates that, "You're wrong." And as more proof he points out that the word "bad" now has a positive connotation in some circles.

"If I say, that was a bad radio show, man, it means it was a good radio show," he says as if he's speaking to a cultural idiot.

"It's different," I say. "The word bad is not racist or anti-Semitic. You can't just change the meaning of racist and anti-Semitic words by wishing it so. Whether you say it or somebody else says them they still get said. And they still have an effect."

My unspoken point is that we call ourselves those words because on some level we feel we are those words and hate being the group that is the target of those words.

I realize that as a Cuban-American man it is possible for me to be more sensitive to the negativity of a Jewish slur than this Jewish man is. And, I realize, it makes me angry. I don't like this guy and his pals "dissin'" themselves. It seems, I'm more upset about this fellow exchanging negatives barbs with his friends than he is.

It just doesn't seem right. It is not appropriate. It is not right. Those words are the destruction of any self-esteem that a culture hopes to give itself. Now, my companion, a lovely lady who belongs to the same group as this fellow, tells me to "calm down" "to not make such a big thing out of it" and that "It doesn't matter what he thinks."

But it does matter. The history of the world is based on people saying things or allowing things to be said "that didn't matter." Hitler in the 1930s. Joe McCarthy in the 1950s. George Wallace in the 1960s. Donald Trump. And in each case, early in their notoriety, it was felt that these people who espoused hateful ideas didn't amount to anything, therefore their ideas didn't amount to anything. They would just disappear if you ignored them.

Wrong. What people say or believe, what people allow other people to say (even in jest) is important. Because what they say are more than opinions — they are beliefs. Words with beliefs behind them hurt — and kill.

Words are an attack against the people who say them even if they are the targets themselves. Only if you think you are a "k-word" or a "n-word" or a "s-word" or all the other hateful, disgusting characterizations of human beings, would you allow someone to say those words to you. The world is not a safe place, attacks can come from all fronts, and the unkindest cut of all is that one that comes from those you thought were safest.

Et tu, Brute.

Europe Remembered

I've traveled in ninety-three countries on hundreds of journeys and had many exciting experiences. Among them I've jumped into the Devil's Pool in Victoria Falls, kayaked past Hippo City in Zambia, climbed to Tiger's Nest in Bhutan, helicoptered over the Matterhorn, dined with famous French winemakers and engaged in a monk chat in Thailand. There is a difference between Eye-Opening, Mind-Blowing experiences like these and Life-Changing ones. Experiences become life-changing when they open your mind to a world of

Other mountains may be taller, but few are more dramatic
than Switzerland's Matterhorn (2012)

possibilities and change your perspective on life. The experience reorders your priorities and alters your path towards fulfilling your potential and giving life meaning. My first European trip in 1969 as part of the UCLA theater troupe did that for me. Since then although I'm blessed with the opportunity to see the world, Europe will always own a piece of my heart.

In January I will be in Europe gathering material for my shows on "Winter in the Alps" — a famous Old World pastime.

I love Europe. I fell in love at first sight. I was 23 in 1969 when the USO gave my fellow UCLA actors and me the opportunity to spend ten weeks entertaining the American troops in Germany.

Europe was different. There was a sense of quality and beauty in ordinary things that I had never seen before. As a young man from a young country I was overwhelmed by the history. So much had occurred there — so many wondrous things — and horrible things.

In my mind's eye I could witness the historic events that had transpired. Europeans exuded a life perspective forged in the fire of their turbulent history and a wisdom honed by the day-to-day survival of generations upon generations.

It was a world I had not known existed. I was pleased and comforted to see that here mankind had suffered all manners of hell and still endured. At the Dachau Concentration Camp I was sickened by man's inhumanity to man, as well as uplifted by man's ability to survive and persist to persevere in the face of unimaginable horrors.

At home the Vietnam War debate was raging. The country was starkly divided between those who supported the President and the war and those who were struggling to end it.

In Vietnam, young Americans were dying in numbers that ultimately added up to more than 58,000. Someday their names would be chiseled into a black granite memorial for all to see and touch. Yet in 1969 they were still out of reach — names in the paper, faces on the news. I met them in Germany. Many we entertained were on their way to 'Nam — and would never go home again. They were homesick boys yearning to return to "The World." They were boys who got teary-eyed when we sang *California Dreaming* and whooped and hollered when any of our Cali gals came out onto the stage.

It was an honor to perform for them, even though I abhorred their mission. As I prepare to return to Europe, I know that I will feel more at home there than I do in the United States right now.

My kinder, gentler, hopeful America is ailing. I fear we have lost our sense of self, our direction and our dedication to create a world that works for everyone. Not just the rich and powerful, but the poor and vulnerable as well. I am discouraged, but I am not defeated. And I expect Europe, with its never-ending celebration of all things human, will soothe and revitalize me.

Jesus of Nazareth said, "In the world ye shall have tribulation: but be of good cheer; I have overcome the world." I'm sticking with that advice.

The Fear of Travel

With spring in the air, my thoughts return to 1980, my last pre-travel writing career journey to Europe. Later that year I would sell my first travel story to the Los Angeles Times for $100. It was a nuts and bolts story relating my experience with Leasing a Car in Europe. This is the trip where my travel obsession became my life and I came face-to-face with the Fear of Travel.

Let's go! Travel! This year, while it's still affordable. London. Paris. The world. Anywhere, as long as it's now! Beautiful cities, exciting adventures and smiling faces beckon to us from ads, articles and brochures. The magnetic attraction is strong. Some of us envision a return to the scenes of past pleasures; others dream of having them for the first time.

With images of past European trips in my head, I could see myself setting foot again on paths I had strolled, tasting the foods that had thrilled me, visiting the places that had never really left my mind. My heart immediately filled with excitement, my taste buds with expectation, and the rest of me with — FEAR!

Yes, fear. Fear of travel — an interesting malady: a

subtle cross between high blood pressure and drowning. Based in our unconscious belief that every silver lining has a cloud, this fear can make the enjoyable tasks of trip preparation practically unbearable.

It begins with thinking that the most important factor to consider when planning a trip is money. I had saved what I felt was sufficient for a five-week vacation for two. So far so good.

It was when I realized that I was actually going to spend the money that the terror struck. It was no longer going to be locked up all cozy in my bank's big, strong vault.

Suppose while we were on vacation, laughing, eating, drinking and dancing our way through the pleasure gardens of Europe, the "Crash of 1980" struck? Returning from our spendthrift ways, we would find the economy in a shambles and a place for me in the unemployment line. Unable to pay the mortgage, I would lose my home. My wife, disgusted at my horrible timing, would leave me for the mail carrier (one of the employed few). My eventual demise

was certain — and all for my brief fling in the European sun.

It also began to strike me at 3 a.m. each morning that there were other things I could do with that money — more important things. Certainly, I had saved it for this trip, but now that I mentioned it, there were things that I wanted more. Like a mountain cabin. (Well, at 3 a.m., it sounded like a good idea.) In lieu of that, I could buy some new clothes, a new car (the '71 Datsun was dying), or maybe a different trip (some place cheaper, like Colorado). Why, I could wear my new clothes while I drove my new car to Colorado. Who needs Europe anyway?

I spent those lonely nights sitting straight up in bed, the sweat pouring off my face, eyes bloodshot and staring wildly into the dark. Eventually, my shaking would awaken my wife, who would assure me that everything would be all right. Obviously, she was not aware of all the things there were to worry about.

What about the house? A house sitter staying in my house filled me with horror. They would probably have wild parties with everyone dancing around on the hardwood floors with taps on their shoes.

They might sneak in a dog! Can you imagine what a dog could do to the hardwood floors — never mind his impact on the cat? What if they didn't like our cat? What if the cat didn't like them? Even worse, what if the cat liked them better than us? There was much to consider.

Although my

demons were going wild, there was still time for the trivial duties of life, such as eating and sleeping. Yet, when we began to work on our itinerary, there was time for nothing else.

Our original plan was to stay in Europe for five weeks. As I worked on the itinerary, the vacation swelled like rice. We were definitely going to England because we speak English, and to France because my wife was studying French. We also had to go to Spain because of my Spanish heritage. And since it is only a flick of a bull's ear to Portugal, we couldn't miss Portugal. And what about Italy and Germany and ... . It wasn't long before our vacation had increased in both weeks and dollars.

My wife had an interesting suggestion. "We don't have to stay so long," she said. "I think just seeing London and Paris would be wonderful." Long pause. What was she trying to do, make things simple?

I moved into action. I used the old "If only we had" technique loved by worriers the world over. If only we had more time, more money; if only we could go here as well as there. Using this argument accompanied by pitiful looks and colorful travel folders, I eventually convinced my wife I could handle seven weeks. That way, we could visit more than I had expected and half of what I desired.

The itinerary planned, reserving our flight became my next challenge. Calling the different airlines was quite an enjoyable experience. True, it took hours and hours, but I received a lot of helpful information and listened to several versions of *Moon River* while on hold.

After being initiated into the mysteries of airline pricing, I finally settled on flying standby. It's inexpensive, and since we were going off-season, we would probably have no trouble getting on. Besides, since standby is a kind of airline Russian roulette, it appealed to the gambler in me.

With the departure date drawing closer, things were looking up. The money was adequate, the house sitter reliable, the tickets paid for.

Unaccustomed to an anxiety-free moment, I quickly found new worries.

Bills, taxes, the mortgage — all had to be paid in advance. Now was the time to fertilize the avocado trees, transplant the roses and put in a new lawn. And if I didn't paint the garage now, later it would be too hot. Or too windy. Or too rainy.

The calm having left me, I began to race against time. Each task done created two new ones. My only hope of keeping a step ahead of the advancing horde was to do more than  one thing at a time. One day, while taking up the front lawn, painting the garage and changing the oil in my car, I was engulfed. "I give up!" I screamed, throwing my shovel into the steer manure. "It's impossible. I can't go. I can't do it all in the time that's left!"

I rushed into the house to give my wife the bad news that we would have to call the airlines, call our friends, cancel all plans, lose all deposits; the trip was off. She would be disappointed, but, of course, she would understand how impossible it was.

I found her asleep on the living room floor, surrounded by maps. Our itinerary lay near her head; a book about castles in Spain was open by her hand; her French lessons were running on the cassette player by her side. *"Bienvenue ... soyez le bienvenu a la belle France ..."* was all I understood: "Welcome, welcome to beautiful France."

Like a spotlight, it hit me. "Hey, fella, you're going to Europe. It's over there; you've been in here. You've closed your eyes to the joys; you've only seen the fears. Open your eyes up and look out."

Tentatively, I looked out. I looked out at my wife, lying there exhausted from all the work she had put into this trip. I looked at the maps around her. I saw France. I saw Spain. There's London. Here's Madrid. I looked at the points my wife had circled and remembered.

In this area, the wine is delicious. Here, we'll stay in a manor that's been an inn for 400 years. In this village, there are cottages with flowers growing out of thatched roofs. The cathedral here took 300 years to build; people worked on it knowing they would never see its end. Here, there's a little farmhouse where the owners gather your breakfast items from their garden that morning. In the river outside this town the fish are plentiful and the old men will show you the best spots. And everywhere, there are museums. Everywhere, art. Everywhere, beauty.

I knelt down beside my wife. My movement wakened her. "What's wrong?" she asked.

"Nothing," I said. "Everything is fine. Everything will wait. We're going to Europe. And we're going together."

"Yes," she said, burying her head in my lap, starting to fall back to sleep. "Isn't it wonderful?"

At that moment, all fear of travel left me. All the anxiety, all the doubts that had clouded my eyes for so long. I saw my wife. I saw those multi-colored maps with all the marvelous places we were going to visit and I thought, "After all, what's a memory worth?"

Home Fires

Christmas Smoke

I'm a second generation American of Cuban heritage. Until the age of five I spoke only Spanish, but my parents were of a generation eager to assimilate into America's white Anglo-Saxon world and insisted that, although they spoke Spanish to each other, their children must only speak English. So I forgot my language and I almost lost my culture. Thankfully, during my childhood I got a sustaining dose of Cuban traditions at my grand-

My maternal grandfather Carlos Lazo and his ever-present cigars (c. 1954)

parents' house. Leaving Florida and going to Los Angeles for graduate school finally freed me to be me. I stopped telling people I was Spanish/Italian and owned up to my Cuban ancestry, which to my surprise was considered exotic in California. Since then I've reveled in celebrating my Cuban roots. I've visited Cuba a half dozen times and every year I recreate my grandparents' Noche Buena (Christmas Eve) Cuban feast at our home.

For me Christmas will always be associated with a pungent cloud of white smoke rising from the glowing end of a long, fat handmade Cuban cigar.

Actually, I would be more accurate if I said, "a long, fat cigar handmade by a Cuban." My grandfather, Carlos Lazo de Lazo, was the undisputed patriarch of my family. He was a Cuban man's man. Silent and strong, boisterous and sentimental, rough and narcissistic, gentle and generous. He was a paradox, as Cuban men tend to be, a combination of many elements and not all of them pleasant.

His immediate family consisted of a doting wife 16 years his junior and four daughters. One, Lolita, died at the age of 21 of Bright's disease. He had no sons.

He had me. I was the first boy born into the family and my grandfather's favorite grandchild. *Machungo*, he would call me. A term that lovingly translates as "Little Macho Man." In this age of male chauvinism and feminism, I'm not embarrassed by the term. Being my grandfather's favorite has stood me in good stead for most of my life. My grandparents taught me about love, my grandfather taught me how to appreciate the finer things in life and that dark, oily, fat *cigarro* was an essential part of the lesson.

If he were here, this is how he might have told me his story ...

"Before leaving Cuba during the Spanish-American War my family owned and farmed a tobacco plantation in the western Cuban province of Pinar del Rio. Besides growing *el mas fino* tobacco in Cuba, we ran a casino on the side. It was a casino in the historic sense — 'a gathering place for social amusements.' There was no gambling (well, maybe an occasional bet on a game of dominos or a cockfight), but plenty of *vino, musica,* dance and cigar smoke.

"I started smoking cigars when I was seven years old and in 1903, when I was 25 years old, I brought the habit and art of cigars with me to the Ybor City quarter of Tampa, Florida. At the Hav-A-Tampa Cigar Company, I refined my talent as a blender of tobaccos to such an extent that when the millionaire Summerfield wanted to start a cigar factory in Miami, he hired me. I brought my family to Miami and so, *chico,* cigars are

responsible for your parents meeting and you and your sisters and brother being born.

"In 1940, I built a concrete block building behind my home on Ninth Street. We called it *el chinchal,* which means "a mom and pop business," but which, to Cubans in Tampa, Miami and Key West, can only mean a small cigar factory. In tribute to the company that gave me my first job in America, I named my company — "Have-A-Miami." Together with your father and my oldest daughter, Blanquita, I peddled my combustibles to the Cuban *tiendas* and *restaurantes* in Miami. Until 1957, I employed between 12 to 25 cigar makers

who each hand-rolled about 100 cigars a day. My family, including my wife, Maria, my daughters and your sisters, put bands and wrappers on the cigars and pressed them into the boxes, being very careful not to break them.

My grandparents Carlos and Maria still clowning around after 45 years (1956)

"*Todo mi vida* I smoked 15 to 20 cigars a day, starting each morning with *un cabo*, a half-smoked cigar saved from the night before, waiting at my bedside. I died in 1963, at the age of 85, *enfermo, si, chico, pero* more sick of living without my Maria, than sick."

Gracias for your story, abuelito.

The image of my grandfather sitting in a rocking chair on his porch with a cigar burning between his fingers is indelibly burnt into my memory. The porch is unscreened, of concrete construction with a low wall and pillars. The furniture consists of my grandparents' rocking chairs and a group of straw-backed chairs that we pulled up next to theirs. My cousins and I would watch the ash on his cigar growing ever longer and wager whether it would tumble down the front of his shirt before he flicked it off. I learned that if I bet on my grandfather, I always won.

The best Christmases of my life took place in or around my grandparents' house. The annual Christmas pageant, directed by my sister, Oneida, and starring "the cousins," was held in my grandmother's living room. The opening of family gifts took place around the fifteen-foot Christmas tree next door in my aunt's boarding house. The traditional *Noche Buena* feast was served in *el chinchal*. Most of the courses — the salad, *yuca* (cassava), black beans, white rice and fried plantains — were prepared in my grandmother's kitchen. But the main course, the roast pig, was my grandfather's sole domain.

He sat in front of a shallow pit dug in the back yard. The pit was filled with 20 pounds of glowing charcoals. Across the pit a flat grill constructed of wire mesh and made to swing, slowly rocked to and fro. Upon the grill a 50-pound pig marinated overnight in sour orange juices and pocked with garlic cloves lay spread eagle, the fat oozing out until it dripped onto the coals with mini-explosions. The weather was invariably warm so that you couldn't tell if the hot on your face came from the coals or the blazing sun. In my grandfather's left hand was a glass of red wine, in his right the ever-present cigar.

Every now and then, with a timing tuned to some infallible inner clock, he nudged the swing in order to keep the pig gently rocking to and fro. Every now and then, he let me rock it. I was tentative, nervous — anxious to please. But after a few tries — this time too hard, that time too gently — I caught the rhythm.

My grandfather spoke little English, and although I understood Spanish, I spoke not a word. So we did not speak. We sat, watched the pig and rocked the swing surrounded by the warmth of the fire and a cloud of cigar smoke. I felt special, I felt like a *machungo*.

So this Christmas, wherever I am and in spite of the United States' 60-year boycott against Cuba, I will toast my grandfather with a glass of *vino tinto* and light up *un Cubano*.

May all our Christmases be merry, but if not merry, at least as pleasurable as the times I spent breathing in my grandfather's smoke and watching the Christmas pig roasting on an open fire.

Gin, Gin – The Dancing Machine

My father and my mother were married for 42 years. I wouldn't say it was a happy marriage, they argued every day of my childhood, but they withstood each other and stayed together. Life was a struggle. My father had a sixth grade education so, in order to raise four kids, he took every part-time and odd job he could. My mother, with an eighth grade education, was "a housewife." She was a quiet introvert; he was a loud extrovert. He wanted to Go-Go-Go and she wanted to Stay-Stay-Stay. That may have been the source of their problems, but I'm sure raising four children with a top

With my parents in the front yard of our Northwest Miami home. (1974)

salary of $5,000 a year (that's about $38,000 in 2020 dollars) added to the stress. He didn't drink or smoke, but he gambled. With no prospects to speak of his only hope for prosperity was to hit the numbers or have his greyhound come in at the Flagler Dog Track. He had an epiphany and quit gambling cold turkey one night, but it was too late for my mom's dreams of a nice home equal to those of her sisters to come true, which created more tension. In any case, with my sisters married with children and my brother and I on our own, when my mother died my dad was like a cork on a champagne bottle. The pressure was off and he was ready to enjoy life free of encumbrances.

Joseph Rosendo, 21, looking sharp and ready to party (1936)

With noticeable pride he told me they called him "Gin, Gin — The Dancing Machine." Most likely they meant "Gene, Gene — The Dancing Machine," after the character on the '70s series, *The Gong Show*. So, it wasn't necessarily a compliment, but he didn't know or care what they called him — he was on an undeclared mission.

Every day for a year after my mother died, my father came home from his job as a custodian at Miami Central High School in Florida, took off his gray uniform with "Joe" stitched on the shirt pocket, put on his pink silk shirt and brown slacks,

206

combed his thinning hair into a slicked back 1940s style and went out.

Where he went was to a local disco, optimistically named *El Paradiso*, which was two blocks away from his home in a rundown neighborhood near downtown Miami. There he drank one or two whiskey sours (he never liked the taste of alcohol), laughed and spoke with all the young couples and swinging singles … and danced. He danced with women twenty, thirty, forty years his junior. In truth, he danced with any woman who would dance with him. Most he asked, agreed to take a spin on the multicolored, flashing floor with "Gin, Gin — The Dancing Machine."

And why not? He was harmless. A short, cute Cuban elf. After fifty years of manual labor packing ice, delivering milk, mowing lawns, selling mangos, cleaning schools and hundreds of other full-time, part-time, and one-day jobs, he was fit, had a winning smile (when his missing molars didn't show), and was filled from his feet to the ends of his wispy salt and pepper hairs with an endless supply of energy. At sixty-two, he had been set free and was ready to party.

But then, ever since I knew him he had been ready to party. Whether it was during my Aunt Maggie's birthday blasts in her cramped apartment above a garage or at the yearly *Noche Buena* Christmas Eve celebrations held at my Aunt Blanca's two-story boarding house and grandfather's cigar factory or as a guest at the wedding receptions of an endless number of first, second and honorary cousins and distant relatives, he was always the first and last on the dance floor.

He danced to all kinds of music — mambo, rumba, merengue, slow waltzes, fox trot, twist, classical. If there were music, he'd find a way to move to it. It didn't matter what that music was because, truly, he danced to the beat of his own drummer.

Gin, Gin — The Dancing Machine competing in the Friday disco night contest at *El Paradiso* in 1975. Yes, of course, he won.

His partners were the paintbrushes he used to make his flamboyant, sweeping strokes across the floor. Trying to keep up with him was more a matter of endurance than talent. His partners invariably left the floor spent, shaking their heads, wiping their brows and, literally, holding their sides laughing. Even those who were not up to the task, who stood stiff as mannequins in his hands and struggled to retain their sense of decorum, had to admit that a dance with *Josie* (my mother's pet name for him) was an exuberant, entertaining experience. He danced with everyone and with no one.

In fact, during his year of release at the *El Paradiso*, he was most happy when he danced by himself. Every Friday night they had a dance contest. That was an opportunity for the real *danseurs* in the crowd to strut their stuff. It was a chance for my father, freed from the constraining bounds of dance steps and other people's toes, to let the stops out.

On the back of a snapshot that he sent me of him whizzing around that flashing rainbow floor he wrote, "Gin, Gin the dancing machine. That's what they call me. Real name, Joseph Rosendo, Your Dad."

Yes, I guess, he was that too.

A Father's Gift

I studied, trained and tried to find work as an actor for fourteen years. The greatest success I had in my acting career was getting cast in the USO show that sent me to Europe. After I came back I was hooked on travel and had the dream of making travel my life. I knew the What and Why of my dream, but I didn't have a clue about the How. Fortunately, at that right moment in my life, I came across this quote from Henry David Thoreau: "If one advances confidently in the direction of their dreams, and endeavors to live the life which they have imagined, they will meet with a success unexpected in common hours." I had my dream and thereafter, most days, I endeavored to live the life I imagined and everything has materialized from those endeavors. It took years, not days, but then, as playwright Edward Albee wrote, "Sometimes you have to go a long way out of your way in order to come back a short distance correctly."

It's holiday time. Thanksgiving, Hanukkah, Christmas, New Year's. A time when most of us polish up our hopes and expectations.

Being young in America was like Christmas for me. I was always hearing that I could be anything I wanted — just work hard enough and wrap the package up in the brightest, shiniest paper you have and your dreams will come true.

President, Businessman, Sportsman, Sailor, Writer, Actor — it's all available. You can be anything you want in the Land of the Free.

Later, I realized what few choices I really had. Considering where I came from and whom I came from, there were really only a few things I could happily become.

And I'm one of them.

I was supposed to become a professional baseball player. My father's dream was to be a baseball player. He never had the chance. He sold newspapers in front of a movie theater during the Depression when he was eight. He went to work for his father, Cheche, in the family butcher shop when he was ten. He did what his father told him to do — and baseball, although it was the American pastime and a Cuban passion, seemed a bit too much like fun to my grandfather. He would have none of that for his children.

Cheche was a killer

My Dad, second baseman for the champion White Belt Dairy softball team (1949)

of dreams. I remember him in his last years sitting on his rocker on his front porch in the dark in order to save money on electricity. He rocked back and forth, never saying a word. As opposed to my mother's father who adored me, my father's father ignored me — and everyone else. He was like a black hole that sucked the oxygen from a room with his stony silence.

He didn't care about my father's dream to be like Lou Gehrig, Babe Ruth and Joe DiMaggio. So, my father gave up his dream and fulfilled his father's for him and became an uneducated, hardworking, manual laborer who would always want more than he could get. He played the numbers and chased the greyhounds. He squandered what little money he had in search of a way out. So it was understandable that my father wanted me to live his dream.

Or did he?

He taught me how to bat left-handed (for that extra step to first base), he pitched the ball to me (and at me) daily, and during my childhood ballgames, stood behind the batter's cage and shouted words of encouragement.

"Watch the ball. Keep your eye on the ball. Nooow, swing! Oh, Christ, you'll never get a hit that way."

He was his father's son.

It's the same with me. Raised as a referee to my parents' battles, my moments in the sun were chiseled out of mountains of anxiousness. And as far as baseball goes, like my father I was too preoccupied with survival to really learn the game. I ran and hit and threw and I tried to please, but my heart wasn't in it. My father's relief when I hung up my glove for good was obvious. In the end, he couldn't have or share his dream.

By accident, he gave me another — travel. Our yearly family vacation consisted of a one-day trip to Key West, Florida, my dad's hometown. It may not seem like much (usually we didn't even stay overnight), but it was a great joy to all of us. It was the one time the quarrels stopped and my parents were pleasant to each other — even loving. They enjoyed the anticipation of good times as well.

The trips were always best at the beginning. When the disappointments had not yet set in and the fantasy was still sweet and fresh. We'd climb into my father's gray Ford station wagon and head down "The Overseas Highway" (US 1) for the end of the road.

We started before the sun came up, filled with excitement and expectation. "We have to beat the heat," my father said when my mother asked why we always had to get up so early.

I still love the feeling of being up before anyone else and on the way to somewhere others would like to go.

The road equaled love. So, you don't have to be a shrink to understand why I became a travel writer — eventually. Considering my history, did I really have any other choice?

Could I really be the movie star I worked so many years to become? Or could I be happy in a company confined to a building that, no matter how multi-national or architecturally beautiful, would always be a trap to me?

I needed the open road. So I crafted my escape. And with a little help from my friends, I create it anew each day. When things are tough, sometimes I wish I could follow a path that someone else must walk first each day. But it's not for me, or rather I'm not for it. I really have no other options.

During my actor days, we spoke about obsession. We said the actors who made it, who could stand the humiliation and rejection, had no other alternatives. For the successful ones, there is no other way. Although the kind of security a salary implies seems attractive, I realized fairly early on that it would offer no security for me. The only "security" I could stand was none at all.

And I thank my father for that. Perhaps, he taught me the false face that security can wear. He taught me that home, family, job are all puzzles that, without notice, can explode into a trillion pieces and, like Humpty-Dumpty, never be put together again.

I am the fulfillment of my history — the natural progression of events and circumstances and motivations. And like my career, I attempt to create myself anew every day.

"The past is prologue," wrote Shakespeare.

It's strange to think that for so long, I was confused as to what direction to travel when, after all, if I had only looked to from whence I came, I would have known which way to turn. I would have known to stop all the thrashing about and embrace my path — not an easy one, maybe, but my own.

Nature Calls

California Highway 27 winds through Topanga Canyon alongside Topanga State Park, the largest wildland within the boundaries of a major U.S. city, and the colorful and historic community of Topanga. The mountain hamlet is home to artists, healers, musicians, educators, naturists, hippies, rustics and my wife, our two cats and me. I discovered Topanga in 1970 when four of us actors from UCLA performed at the first Topanga Days festival. With its cliffs, canyons, native oaks and soaring pines I felt transported to the High  *Sierra. Protecting and preserving this treasure is a full-time job Topangans have worked at for generations. Our motto is: "Don't Change Topanga, Let Topanga Change You." Nevertheless, from corporate developers and highway*

217

engineers to new arrivals trying to be nature proof, there's a long list of forces attempting to urbanize, sanitize and otherwise change Topanga's natural landscape and unique spirit. Their "good intentions" frequently result in ecological and scenic devastation. I've lived in Topanga since 2007 and feel pretty passionate about it.

God has cared for these trees, saved them from drought, disease, avalanches, and a thousand tempests and floods. But he cannot save them from fools.

John Muir

They are cutting down the pine trees in Topanga. Pines that have thrived here for more than fifty years and transformed the native Southern California shrub forest into a high country woodland are now being reduced to garden mulch. Some of these monarchs had sprouted of their own accord in Southern California's Mediterranean climate and others Topangans planted at the urging of the Fire Department in order to grip the soil that clings to our hillsides. They are now deemed of little worth.

Fear-induced, money-driven public policies that target them as non-natives and fire-hazards have created boatloads of cash that is being used by slyly named "Fire Safe Councils", supported by the aforementioned Fire Departments, to convince (some say coerce) homeowners into chopping them down.

Fear and money talks and presented with the horrors of blazing infernos, threats of liability and the costs of removing such a magnificent godly construction, frightened and budget-conscious homeowners have agreed with the insidious bureaucratic plan.

How can they do it? How can man whose feet are anchored to the earth ruthlessly end the lives of beings whose only desire is to touch the sky? How can earthbound man contain and control that eternal heavenly striving? How does it happen that in the course of their manipulated lives man can so carelessly interrupt the instinctive ones that surround them?

We have less oxygen now, less beauty and less majesty — and less wildlife too. The great horned owls that lived in the pine branches fifty, seventy-five and hundred feet above the ground and called to each other and serenaded us in the night are gone.

In my bed, I am awakened by what I do not hear. I feel alone and abandoned. And as I am slowly sinking into a painful awareness of the new silence, in the distance I discern the calls of coyotes. Masters of adaption they have weathered every man-made intrusion and continue to survive in Topanga State Park.

Living on the edge of the parklands as we do, we are sometimes graced by their high-pitched cries. I rise and go out into the cool Topanga night so that I can better hear their yips and yelps. So I can better divine what they are chattering about.

The fearful say that coyotes let out a hue and a cry when they have cornered a prey in order to bring the pack to the feast. Of course, these are the same people who see my glorious pines as torches, which infringe on illusions of safety and threaten dreams of immortality. I think (and there is zoological evidence which supports my thoughts) that the coyotes' exuberant exclamations are shouts of recognition and squeals of joyful reunion.

Whatever their purpose, tonight their yapping comforts me. They remind me that in spite of some of my neighbors' attempts to crush nature, it will survive. And so, under the branches of my towering pines (four of the few remaining in the canyon), I return to, if not an untroubled sleep, a more peaceful one.

The Big Trip

Forever
Journey's End
A Prayer Revisited
Ave Maria
Our Town

Forever

I've realized that since I never know where the next bit of wisdom will come from I should always give people a chance to speak their mind. Just because I realize this, doesn't mean I always practice what I preach. In my family we seem to wait for the other guy to finish their sentence, but, in fact, we're chomping at the bit and expecting the speaker to stop jabbering so we can chime in. Usually, the urge to share our opinion wins out and the conversation escalates into an

Making new friends on Playa Ancon near Trinidad, Cuba (2017)

exercise in topping one another. Often the pace, volume and blood pressures rise so high that we can't even hear each other. Since, as my wife has pointed out, this behavior tends to interfere with listening, I've tried to monitor it with varying degrees of success. I was feeling pretty hopeless about it until I went to Cuba and discovered that's how everyone there communicates. And, strangely enough, it works. So, although it looks like I'm psychic when I finish my wife's statements, I'm merely a victim of my genes and following an ingrained cultural code. Nevertheless, I understand it can be irritating to non-Cubans and it has led me to jump to some unfortunate conclusions.

"Enjoy Yourself (It's Later Than You Think)"
Carl Sigman & Herb Magidson, 1949

"I'm dying," Ed tells me during lunch at a swank Santa Monica restaurant.

I'm dumbstruck. What can I say? How do I reply to a friend who has just mentioned the unmentionable, the unexplainable and the unthinkable — Death?

"We've got to hurry up and finish that video project because I'm dying."

I'm horrified. Ed has a wife and three children. They depend on him. Hell, I depend on him to make me laugh and rev up my creativity.

Finally I recover my voice. "I'm sorry," I whisper. "What—are—you—dying—of?"

"Life," he says, "I won't get out of it alive. Will you?"

I groan. "You jerk." Then I laugh — a bit too loudly. "That was a good one. You really had me going."

It's a joke. He's not really dying. I'm relieved, but, strangely enough, not comforted. And Ed? He's not laughing.

Not really dying? Who am I kidding? Just me, of course.

Of course, Ed is dying. Of course, we're all dying and, yes, it's best we do what we want to do sooner rather than later.

It's a New Year. Time sprints on and I can't seem to make it put on the brakes. Thank goodness, I live in Los Angeles where there are no real seasons. The changing seasons highlight the passage of time. I already have a calendar in my desk's bottom drawer that does the same thing, thank you.

Tempus Fugit. Time flies and nothing I can do will stop it. No matter how many prayers I say, parties I attend, hours I work, things I buy, the day will still become night without asking me for help. One year flips over to the next, one season melds into the following — one white hair joins another and a wrinkle finds a friend.

So, how can I slow this inexorable movement to the end?

I can't.

Webster has a definition to offer:

Forever *(n): An interminable time. (adv): For a limitless time.*

It seems nothing is forever, but forever.

Of all the things that pass quickly, good times

pass the fastest. A visit to the dentist seems to take forever, a divorce takes forever, getting the proverbial "check in the mail" takes forever, but all the enjoyable things in life pass quickly. My father used to say, "All good things come to an end." I think I became a travel writer in order to make good things longer lasting.

Now maybe this isn't a problem for others. Maybe they can squeeze into a two-week vacation so much pleasure that it satisfies them. It's enough for them. It's not enough for me. I need more — more time, more experiences — more.

My hunger for more was fed to me with my mother's milk. My mother was never satisfied — wherever she was. She was always ready to move on. Throughout my entire childhood whenever we went someplace — be it the yearly family picnic at Miami Beach, the New Year's Eve parade on Biscayne Boulevard or a visit to my sister's home in South Miami — we would arrive early and once there my mother was ready to leave. She wanted to be somewhere else. Perhaps what we thought was impatience was restlessness, wanderlust. Maybe I became a travel writer in order to keep on moving on.

Mostly it seemed a good way to make the enjoyable things in my life become my life. The 17th century poet Robert Herrick said, "Gather ye rosebuds while ye may." I've heard people say, "If I stopped and gathered all the roses I wanted I would never do anything else." Yet maybe his roses aren't roses at all, but brightly colored fragrant experiences.

Life is too short for doing anything but enjoying being alive. It's our number one job. There are no other worthy occupations.

"So, Joseph," I said to myself. (My therapist tells me it's all right to talk to yourself as long as you don't answer.) "You love travel, so why not do it all the time?" And for 40 years I have. When I start to complain about what I do and begin to think that traveling is tough and the money not enough — when I begin to salivate after the big house on the hill or the shining Mercedes on the road, I remind myself that it's hard to be rich and there are untold prices to pay. And, "Let's face it, Joseph (there I go again), you never wanted to work that hard or to pay those prices anyway."

I can't stop time. I can't slow it down or extend it. And no one can guarantee me that I have more than one life to live. So, it's "Love it and Live it or Lose it." All things (not just good things) come to an end and it is truly over before we know it and it is later than we think. It's a bitch, but that's the way it is. Hey, but who's got the time to waste complaining? We're all dying, aren't we?

Journey's End

Now that I'm old it's clear that my life has been driven by chance and choice. First of all there are the many times I dodged death. To my surprise, I've discovered there are quite a few of them. I'm thankful and grateful the powers-that-be granted me a pass and gave me the opportunity to get older and wiser. Then there are the milestones that marked my journey to this time and place. There were many, here are a few: Not taking the parole officer job in Miami and going to graduate school in California. Accepting the role in the USO show that sent me to Europe. Going to the seminar in San Diego, which convinced me to become a travel writer. In the middle of a divorce, answering the heavenly call to create a non-existent television show. Meeting my wife Julie while covering a fundraiser for her PBS station in San Antonio. Living in Topanga. These were some of the forks in the road I encountered and I'm glad that, more often than not, I followed Robert Frost's advice and "took the path less traveled." Yet, one choice most of us don't get to make is when and where we'll die. No matter when it happens, I'm pretty sure the timing will suck, so my only consolation is to live fully now. Or as the Greek philosopher and dramatist Seneca put it more than two thousand years ago, *"Life is a play. It's not its length, but its performance that counts."*

> *Do not go gentle into that good night.*
> *Rage, rage against the dying of the light.*
>   Dylan Thomas

A friend died today. She was in her early sixties and although she had never smoked a cigarette, she battled lung cancer for two years. Until near the end, only her family knew she was sick.

Donna Carroll

At first, that angered me. She was our friend and we only had a month to express our love. And then I realized that her family had given her friends time enough to "pay their respects." They knew that a month of pampering, pandering and fawning was about all she could stand. Waiting to share the intimacy of her illness had allowed her to live as she always had. She had decided that, in the words of Dylan Thomas, "death shall have no dominion" over her life.

The doctors had originally predicted six months, but she had lived fully for two years. Even so, the family knew that when the quality of her life deteriorated enough, she would not want to go on anymore. She would not put up with the "nonsense."

The "nonsense" of being spoon-fed and unable to walk. The "nonsense" of being too tired to talk, wear her stylish clothes, drive her red sports car, socialize and travel. She was and is — her images burn on — a respected travel photographer. She had traveled the world with her camera, her writer husband and, when they were small, her children.

I was always envious of Donna and Richard. Among the many ups, one of the downs of being a travel writer is that if your significant other is not in the business, you are often in the most beautiful places on the planet — alone. I have been in spots so excruciatingly romantic that I had to leave. It was too painful being there by myself.

You see, for me, travel is a shared experience. I want someone with whom to share sunrise on Machu Picchu, nights on the Mediterranean, the stones and stories of Jerusalem and all those plush king-size beds, in-room jacuzzis and scrumptious dinners. Often it's a struggle to make a living as a travel journalist. Yet, most of us don't do it for money, we do it for love — love of adventure, of experience, of people and, above all else, as an expression of love of another.

So, I was envious of the Carrolls. They were a team in life, in work and in travel. And they didn't wait to travel until their children left, they didn't wait until retirement, they didn't wait until there was only time to eke out a few exhausted trips before one of them said a last "good night." They wandered together for more than forty years — from living out of a car in France and camping with the kids in Mexico to hobnobbing with the rich and famous on a Grand Princess cruise — they did it all — and they did it together.

Now, that may sound hellish to some. "Work and play together? I couldn't stand it," they say. "The stress of travel <u>and</u> togetherness. It'll kill a relationship." Well, it sounded like heaven to me. The Carrolls were my role models on how a travel writer's life could be, should be and, if I worked hard enough and looked long enough, how it would be for me. But then, the Carrolls didn't have a relationship; they had a love affair for forty-three years.

The day after we heard of Donna's illness, my wife and I went to visit her, commiserate with Richard and try to understand. The last time we saw her, she was at a press luncheon chatting animatedly with a colleague. She was dressed in a smart frock with tiny blue flowers and had a glass of champagne in her hand. She looked great.

This time we found Donna in bed, unable to walk, numbed by painkillers, bald, but still filled with a will to participate and the grace to laugh at herself.

"How do you like my new hair?" she snickered, pointing at her wig on the dresser.

At one point during our visit, Donna asked to get out of bed, and joined us in her den for a beverage and a snack. While the others prepared the food and drink, for a brief moment, I was alone with her.

"So, Donna, what do you think about all this?" I asked.

"I think it sucks, Joe," she said. "It sucks. I'm not ready for this — not now."

I didn't know what to say, except to agree.

"You're right. It sucks."

I thought for a moment and in that moment I looked around her den. The walls, the floors, the bookcases were decorated and filled with artifacts from her travels. There were paintings from Mexico, a wood carving from Africa, a musical instrument from Malaysia and a hand woven rug from the Middle East.

There were books from everywhere, about every place, and above all, there were her photographs.

"It sucks big time, Donna," I finally said. "But, you know, in this room there are a lot of beautiful things from exotic places — works of art, crafts, images. They make the room look beautiful, but they do more. They speak about you. They reflect the life of a person who has seen, known and shared much. In this room, I feel the weight and depth of who you are. And in the end, I guess, it's all we get of life — what we make of ourselves."

She smiled, and we sat in silence.

"Thank you, Joe," she finally said. "It's nice of you to say that."

"It's true," I replied.

"It still sucks," she said.

"Yes," I said, "it still does."

At that moment, Richard entered the room followed by my wife and the rest of Donna's family. I watched her participate in the evening as much as she could. She drank a glass of "terrific" California Chardonnay and munched on a "tasty" hamburger. Always health conscious, burgers were a luxury she did not normally allow herself. This night, she relished it.

She requested flan for dessert, and persuaded my wife and I to drink sparkling wine from the gold-rimmed champagne glasses they had recently used when they renewed their vows on the Grand Princess.

We didn't speak alone again, but at the memorial service two weeks later, our conversation is what I remembered. The service was elegant and joyous. "A celebration of life," Richard called it. Her son shared tender and hilarious family intimacies with a confidence and ease that honored both his parents. A few friends remembered and the pastor eulogized.

During her eulogy, the pastor said that although it was obvious Donna was none too pleased with her lot, "she found peace and acceptance in the end and was ready to go."

That's not the Donna I saw. I saw weariness, maybe, but no acceptance, no resignation. She may have agreed to leave, but she did not go gentle into that good night.

As human beings, our greatest weakness and our greatest strength is our will to survive and our ability to adapt. In order to survive, we can adapt to most anything — including some things we should never agree to adapt to.

Sometimes when the going gets tough, it's not time to get going, but just time to go. Yet, our will to live is so great, we often need permission to let go, to stop adapting to the unthinkable.

Of course, it was Richard who gave Donna the thumbs up. And once given the A-OK for lift off, she went her way. The pastor was wrong; Donna didn't accept her destiny, she accepted Richard's permission. Blessed are the permission givers for they shall set us free.

It reminded me of my brother.

In 1987, at the age of 35, he lay in a morphine-induced coma dying of AIDS in a San Francisco

Ron on San Francisco Bay. He loved the city and was free and at home there for 15 years. (1987)

235

hospital. His breathing sounded incredibly painful as he labored to survive. As I got ready to leave for the night, I put my hand on his head to say goodbye.

"It's all right, Ron," I whispered in his ear, not knowing if he could hear. "It's all right. You've struggled enough. You've suffered enough. We love you. You can go now. It's okay."

Suddenly, his breathing changed. It became more regular; more relaxed — more peaceful, if you will. By the next morning, he had passed on. I had offered him permission to go and he had trusted me enough to take it. It was his final act of brotherly love. His final gift to me. At Donna's memorial, I remembered that and was comforted.

They say people die the way they live. I'm proud of Donna and Ron. They did not go gentle into that good night, they raged, raged against the dying. And they honored us by letting us help them turn out the light.

A Prayer Revisited

I wrote this more than 20 years ago. It's tragic that more than two decades later the opening paragraph basically still applies. As the French say, "Plus ça change, plus c'est la même chose." The more things change, the more they remain the same. This piece is also illustrative of a time when I was being divorced and my ecumenical spiritual journey had led me to a place where the truths of many faiths rang in my ears. The Buddhist belief that in life pain is inevitable, but suffering is optional was certainly timely. As was the advice to be totally engaged, but unattached to the outcome. During those days even the familiar prayers of my father acquired new meaning.

It's the holiday season and as I sit down to write the Israelis and Palestinians are fighting each other in the streets of the Holy Land. In Africa, one side is killing the other with machetes. On the streets of our cities, children are killing each other with handguns.

Although I'm not normally a religious man, I think it's time for a prayer. So, I thought I'd share with you a popular one that I've heard a million times, but just recently understood.

The LORD is my shepherd; I shall not want.

When I was a kid, I thought this line meant that God was the boss and I shouldn't ask him for anything. I should have known better, since I went to church every Sunday with my father. He was Catholic. I wasn't. I was baptized a Methodist because my aunt wanted to be my godmother. That was the last time I was ever in a Methodist church.

My mother was not religious, but my father went to church every day. He got his religious fervor from his mother. She was exceedingly religious. She certainly needed the comfort because her husband was a tyrant.

Whenever we visited her in the evening we would find her in her bedroom praying in front of a little altar she had set up on her dresser. It was very dark in her room, but rows of burning candles on the dresser top illuminated the altar of saints' pictures and rosary beads and a huge picture of Jesus hanging on the wall. A white Jesus with flowing hair was looking down on us, opening his robe and revealing his bright red, burning sacred heart. It scared the hell out of me. Perhaps, that's what it was supposed to do.

Contrary to what I thought as a kid, recently, I've realized the line really means that I needn't fear. God will give me everything I need.

He maketh me to lie down in green pastures;
He leadeth me beside the still waters.

As I child I felt coercion behind those words. All that "making me" and "leading me" really bothered me. It reminded me of the times my father would force me to do something that I didn't want to do, whether it was to play baseball or kiss his ancient aunt with the hairy lip or be quiet or obey him for the hell of it. And although following him could sometimes be fun, most often it just led me to do something that made him unhappy. And when he was unhappy, he made sure I was too.

The green pastures sounded good, but I worried that if I lay in the grass in my clean pants I'd get grass stains on them — which would make my mother none too pleased. I liked water, but my waters were the Atlantic Ocean crashing on Miami Beach. I wasn't too sure what "still waters" were except maybe the stagnant canal behind my sister's house in South Miami that smelled so bad.

Just recently, I've learned that the line means God wants the best for me. That he wants me to prosper and have peace.

He restoreth my soul; He leadeth me in the path of
righteousness for His name's sake.

When I was a kid, the only people who spoke about souls were priests and old ladies. Souls were something you lost to the devil by thinking dirty thoughts. And since for much of my youth all I did was think dirty thoughts, the whole idea of souls, restored or otherwise, frightened me. In fact, I thought that line meant God was storing souls away. I knew about the souls trapped in Purgatory, so I guessed that's where he was keeping them. Righteous was something I could never be, and something the adults were all the time. As far as his name went, I knew I shouldn't take it in vain.

I now know the line means God has an interest in me. He's interested in my deflated self and gloomy moods. He's interested in rekindling my spirit and renovating my dreams like a new room at the Paris Ritz and making it shine like the brass at the Beverly Hills Hotel. And he does this because it pleases him.

> *Yea, though I walk through the valley of the*
> *shadow of death, I will fear no evil:*
> *for Thou art with me;*
> *Thy rod and Thy staff they comfort me.*

As a kid, this was the scariest part of the entire 23rd Psalm. Just imagining walking through a dark graveyard with death hovering in the wings had me trembling in my shoes. It's probably a cultural thing, but my mother loved telling us scary stories. For years, my bedtime story was the synopsis of the old movie, *The Beast with Five Fingers*. It's about a pianist who is murdered and has his hands cut off. The hands wander the night in search of the murderer. "El mano, El mano, The Hand, The Hand is coming," she would whisper from the other room. This was my mother's way of getting us into bed with the blankets over our heads. I knew I wasn't supposed to be afraid because thou was with me, but from what I knew about my father's way with a rod and a staff, I never felt comforted.

What I understand now is that I spent a lot of my life in a valley with the shadow of death hanging over me. I worked in places where getting something done was about overcoming obstacles. I had relationships where success was threatening. I was very adept at bobbing and weaving my way through the valley. I used all my wits and wiles to get me through it and I got through. But I've spent a good chunk of my life fearing evil and expecting that it would crush me at any moment. But I don't feel alone anymore, and the evil is powerless. Love, strength and confidence are the rod and staff that comfort me.

Thou preparest the table before me
in the presence of mine enemies;
Thou anointst my head with oil; my cup runneth over.

As a kid I didn't understand why anyone would want to dine with someone who hates them. I was smarter than I thought. About the rest, I just had visions of my hair plastered down with Brylcreem and spilling a glass of milk on the table, which was something I did on a regular basis.

The truth is that this is the most profound line of all. I see now that the feast is us. We are the feast and God has laid out the riches of our life, we're dressed in our tux and black tie in front of folks who do not have our best interests at heart. And even though we ask them to share it with us, they want to spoil our feast. Yet, we need not be afraid for the abundance of the feast overwhelms them and they have no power to harm, no ability to steal the meat from the table. We can celebrate our blessings in the presence of our enemies because they are rendered powerless by our confidence and strength of character. And, indeed, life itself is such a blessing that our cup runneth over.

> *Surely goodness and mercy shall follow me*
> *all the days of my life;*
> *and I will dwell in the house of the LORD forever.*

When I was a kid living in anyone's house except my own would have been a mercy. So, although the LORD scared me, moving away from my family sure sounded sweet.

Now I know that the house of the Lord dwelleth within each of us — and surely that is goodness and mercy and happiness and peace. It's something I wish for the Israelis, the Palestinians, the people in Africa, my family, my wife, myself and you and yours.

Have a joyous and peaceful holiday, won't you?

Ave Maria

My mother's father, Carlos Lazo, came to the United States in 1898 after the Cuban War of Independence, known in the U.S. as the Spanish-American War. From his home in Pinar del Rio province, where his family had a tobacco plantation and he learned the art of blending tobacco, he traveled to Tampa, Florida to work at the Hav-A-Tampa cigar factory. My grandmother, Maria Milord, was already there. Although much of her history is lost, we know she was born in Key West in 1894, the 24th of her father Domingo's 24 children and her brother was a Cuban consul in Miami. Domingo was also in the cigar business and moved his family to Tampa. My grandparents met there and in 1911, Carlos married Maria, who was 16 years younger, and had four girls. Opportunity knocked and my grandfather took his craft and family to

Miami. He ran a small cigar factory behind their home off Ninth Street and Miami Avenue. My grandmother turned the second floor and attic into a boarding house for select Cuban gentlemen. She did the vetting, cleaned their rooms, made their beds and, occasionally, cooked for them. These were clean and sober Cuban men in need of a room for a night, a week or a month: Jai Alai players, musicians (Desi Arnaz slept there), actors, merchant marines and other new arrivals on their way to a better life. My grandmother's house was a home away from home and she was a mother away from mother. For twelve years of my life la casa de mi abuelita was a center of love, joy and adventures. Every significant celebration of my childhood took place there: Christmas and Thanksgiving, sure, but also, wedding receptions, birthdays and anniversaries were observed in her large living room or in my grandfather's cigar factory. Everyone loved Maria and nobody loved her more than me. While my parental relationships were problematic, my relationship with my "Wita" was filled with unconditional love. I still miss her.

What's up? It's too early. Is it time to leave for Key West for our family annual one-day vacation? Are my brother and me joining Dad and heading out to South Beach for our regular sunrise swim? Why are all these people here? It's the middle of the night. There are my cousins, Jeannie and Bobby. And here's my aunt Gloria and uncle Robert, standing in our living room speaking hurriedly, but quietly with my mom. What's all this bi-lingual mumbo-jumbo about?

"Get up, Joey," my mother says. "Get up and get dressed. We're going to Wita's house."

Through a drowsy mist, I smile. A warm glow envelops me. "Wita's house." My abuelita's house. My grandma's house. This is happy news. I love my grandmother.

I just saw her this evening at a wedding reception for my godfather Joe's friend Julio. She was smiling and laughing and even dancing, which was a "No, No" at this conservative Southern Baptist celebration. Yet, someone brought 45s for the record player and given a chance, Cubans will dance.

I didn't dance. As ten and twelve-year-olds my cousins and I spent the evening running around the church hall, which was decorated with colored crepe paper, helium-filled balloons and, since Christmas was just two weeks away, holiday garland. We spent the night shouting, "You're It!" and running around and about the round tables of family, distant relatives and strangers.

"Who's getting married?" asked my cousin Bobby. "Dunno," I replied. "A friend of Joe's to some skinny American girl."

Who or why didn't matter. It was a party and we were all invited. As a point of honor, my father accepted all invitations to drink, which he rarely did, eat, which he did constantly, and dance, which he loved more than eating and drinking. Years later he prided himself on being the Latin version of "Gene, Gene — The Dancing Machine" from the 70's *The Gong Show*.

"They better have food," my dad complained as my parents dressed in their bedroom.

Since there was no door, their bedroom arguments and discussions came through to us loud and clear. Years later I wondered, "Where did they make the four of us? Standing up in the bathroom?"

They spoke Spanish to each other and English to us. As first-generation Americans they wanted us to assimilate into Miami's Anglo-American culture as soon as possible and, I think, they thought by speaking Spanish they were keeping something from us. We, of course, understood every word they said.

"It's a Baptist wedding," he added. A devout Catholic, I could actually hear his lip curl.

"*Si*," my mother replied, "It is a Baptist wedding. And the girl's family are Americans so there will be no music, no drinking and," she said almost pleading, "no dancing ... but, they'll have food."

"*Coño*. Damn it, they better have food or we're not staying," he replied, picking out the brightest and widest tie in his wardrobe of over-the-top accessories. A dapper gigolo wannabe in his twenties, in his forties, he still felt he could make the cut.

Well, there was music and, yes, there was dancing. My Dad ignored the frowns of my sister Oneida, also a Southern Baptist, and went ahead and "cut a rug."

There also was a cornucopia of the usual "fill 'em up" wedding fare on the buffet table: salads, cold cuts, chunks of yellow cheese, Cuban bread, bowls of potato chips and Lipton soup onion dip and buckets of greasy, gooey potato salad, which my grandmother loved, but, according to my aunt, she should never eat.

"It's bad for your heart, " my aunt Tia warned. "Tia" translates as "Aunt" in Spanish, which nicely illustrates the double-barreled power of my Tia Blanca's family edicts. They were law, but my grandma could wiggle out of any restraints and tonight she ate, drank and danced in celebration of the wedding couple.

My cousins and I spent the reception darting in and out through the long buffet lineup of wedding guests piling pieces of this and slices of that on their plates. During one of our forays I passed my abuelita, who was standing in the line speaking to some relative.

You could tell she was having a good time. Her gold teeth were sparkling. You could only catch the glimmer of her golden teeth when she was smiling expansively.

My grandmother Maria had plenty of gold in her mouth, a testament to mid-20th century dentistry and her penchant for standing out in a crowd. When she talked animatedly, arms waving this way and that, or laughed heartily she and her teeth lit up the room.

My abuelita Maria in 1950. This is how I knew and remember her.

She reached out to me as we scampered by.

"*Mi'jo*," she said. "My son."

I looked back for a second. I can still see the smile on her face and hear the ask in her voice, but I was in a hurry. I was running; going nowhere, just running, running, running.

She wanted a hug. If I had thought to stop, I would have happily complied. I loved to hug my Wita. Only 64, she still smelled of another age. Most often her scent was gardenias and I reveled in the warm, soft, comforting love of her arms. Her hair was done up in curls for the wedding. An elegant Latin lady, she loved to dress up and she loved parties. Her *Noche Buena*, Christmas Eve, Cuban feasts were legendary.

Her hand ran across my face as I scooted by. Bright red nails lightly caressed my cheek asking me to linger, but I slipped away.

"Ow! Wita scratched me," I told my cousin, laughing as we ran on.

It was the last time she touched me.

In a stupor of sleep I dress in my brother's and my room under the glare of the single bare light bulb while my mother and aunt continue to furtively whisper together as if they have a secret. My aunt has a message to deliver. She can't call ahead because we don't have a phone. The only way messages are conveyed to the Rosendos is in person.

Or they can call the Greers next door. My mother hates the sight of the Greers walking across our front yard. It means something bad has happened and it reminds her she's poor. Embarrassed that in Miami,

Florida at the end of the 1950s we don't own a phone, she always says as the Greers trudge their way across our lawn, *"Me da vergüenza hablar con ellos."* "I'm ashamed to speak with them."

Rather than call, this time my aunt, uncle and cousins feel the need to drive the fifteen miles from their home in North Miami to ours in downtown Miami to relay a message and as we all climb into my uncle's 1951 Ford "Woody" Wagon and head to grandma's house, I still didn't know what the message is.

The car is silent. No one says anything, a very uncharacteristic moment in my family history. In conversation we always strive to cram in as many words as we can into as short a space of time as possible. And it is obligatory that when a person finally takes a breath the person they're speaking to jumps in and speaks faster and louder than them.

Not tonight. Still in a daze I look at Jeannie and smile. She's my favorite cousin and it's good to see her. She doesn't smile back. No one's smiling. And for the first time since being swept up into this whirlwind of uncertainty it dawns on me that something's not right and maybe won't be again.

After all these years, I still can't figure out why I didn't figure it out earlier. There is a tempest of activity, yes, but how do I miss it? Maybe, I am stuck in a bubble. Maybe, I'm so accustomed to my family's ongoing chaos, clamor and drama that the strangeness of the moment just washes over me as "nothing new." Or maybe, I don't want to know *que pasa?*

As I sit scrunched up on the back seat of the station wagon alongside my cousins and my little brother, it still doesn't sink in that my life is about to change.

"I told her not to eat the potato salad," aunt Gloria says, shaking her head.

"It wasn't the potato salad," answers uncle Robert. "You know she's been sick a long time."

My mother begins to quietly weep.

"Leluca, don't do that. *Los niños*. Remember the children," my aunt hisses. And then, "I hope she's not dead yet," she adds, joining her sister in tears.

Dead? What? She? Who she? What dead? Who are they talking about? Potato Salad? What Potato Salad? Who's dead? Not my abuelita? Oh. No. Not my abuelita.

"Please, God," I pray.

From the back seat of the wagon I slip to my knees on the car's floor and pray. It's the first, but not my last time.

"Please, please, don't let her die, God, not my Wita. Please, God. I'll do whatever you want, but please, don't let her die."

My twelve-year-old heart wants to stop the pain and desperation I'm beginning to feel. So, I plead with the old bearded super-man to stop time, bring back yesterday and make it all right again.

Suddenly, I realize that my grandmother can die. I never thought that possible before. I can't have that happen. I can't lose people.

"She's not dead," I cry. My aunt and uncle will make it all right.

"Gloria, Robert, you don't know she's dead. She's not dead, right?" I ask. "She's sick, but not dead, right?"

"Yes, Joey" they say, finally, "We don't know she's dead. She could still be alive."

The drive lasts forever. We drive past buildings I don't see and through traffic lights my uncle ignores. I don't really know where I am. I ask over and over, "Is Wita alive?" They refuse to answer. If they aren't filled with tears, their eyes are empty.

As we pull to the curb the flashing blue and red lights from the ambulance shatter the night in front of my grandmother's house and the sight of Tia running toward us, crying and frantically directing us to her house next door, lets me know that nothing's all right. My Wita, my abuela, my abuelita, my grandmother is gone. What I feel is beyond sad. It's unbearable, unbelievable and what "heartbroken" means.

The rest of that night is a blur. A night of sorrow, anger and pain. A night of chaos, confusion and fear. I've never seen adults this out-of-control. They're wailing and weeping. My grandfather Carlos is on the floor, crying out, "Mama, Mama don't leave me."

My father finally arrives from wherever he's been. He read the note my mother hung on our front door. And while he has a love-hate relationship with my grandparents, tonight he faces the reality of Maria's passing and weeps like a baby — like the rest of us.

My grandmother's was the first death in my family. There were others deaths to come — my brother, my parents, my friends — only hers was when I learned that nothing lasts forever, especially the people you love and who love you.

When will my grandchildren learn that truth? Will I be the one that teaches them? In a way, it would be an honor. My grandmother's death is etched in my memory and she will never really die. I've carried her with me for more than sixty years, celebrating her life by keeping her memory alive. She gave me much while she lived and much when she died. Her death was a signpost, a milestone that said: Grow Up.

My grandmother Maria's favorite song was *Ave Maria* and they played it at her funeral service back in 1958, which I did not attend. In 2019, on the exact day of the 61st anniversary of her death, I heard Perry Como sing it over the Christmas station on my car's satellite radio while I waited in line for fuel. I like to think my abuelita tuned it in just for me.

It's a sweet hymn, adapted from Luke 1:28: "And the angel came in unto her and said, 'Hail, thou that art highly favored, the Lord is with thee; blessed art thou among women.'"

In Latin, *Ave* means "Be Well or Farewell." So, now, when I think of my grandma who was blessed among women, I can say, "*Ave Maria*. Farewell, Wita. Wherever you are, be well and know I'll always love you." I'm not very religious, but as far as prayers go — that works for me.

Our Town

I became an actor because my sister Oneida, who is four years older than me, led the way. Not only did she produce, direct and write all of the little Christmas pageants that she roped my cousins and me into performing for the relatives, she pursued her theatrical dream through high school and beyond. She was talented, beautiful and our star — and sometimes I got to help her memorize her lines. In her senior year she played Juliet in Shakespeare's Romeo and Juliet and caught the eye of a Broadway producer. She was on her way to New York when she decided to chuck it all and marry a fellow the family disapproved of and have four children. I had caught the drama bug from her, so I picked up the baton and ran with it. I never regretted becoming an actor. It taught me about people, to relish the moment and appreciate the drama in life.

My 17-year-old sister heading to a dance recital

"It tickles," she said.

"What tickles?"

"It tickles when you rub my leg like that."

"When I massage your leg, it tickles?" he said.

"Not when you massage it, when you grab my knee like you do and rub it — it tickles."

"It shouldn't tickle — it should be sexy," he said.

"Well, it isn't sexy when you grab my knee cap and squeeze," she said.

"I didn't squeeze," he said.

"Yes, you did," she said.

"I didn't," he said.

"Okay," she said, "You didn't — but it felt like you did."

The air was thick surrounding their conversation.

Finally, he said, "I didn't mean to squeeze your knee cap. How would you like me to touch your knee? Like this," he said, running his hand quickly across her leg.

"No," she said, "That's not anything."

"Well, I'm just trying to figure out what you want. Is that what you want?" he asked.

"Don't make fun of me," she said.

"I'm not," he said, making fun of her, "I'm just trying to figure out what you want."

"I want you to touch me without grabbing me — I want you to feel me without feeling me up," she said.

"Okay," he said.

There was a moment of silence while he tried to figure out what she wanted, and if what he wanted was what she wanted. There was a moment of silence while she tried to decide if what he wanted was what she wanted.

After the silence, he said, "You know we will never be like this again."

"What?" she said.

"Never," he said, "We will never be like this again — exactly. Time passes and the moment moves on. We'll never be like this again."

"Yes," she said, hoping that he would stop now.

"You know," he said not stopping, "There's this play by Thornton Wilder. It's an old play written a long time ago about people in a small town. In fact, it's called *Our Town*."

"Yes," she said.

"I was just a kid when I first read it. Are you still awake?"

"Yes," she said, her eyelids becoming heavy.

"I was just a kid, maybe eleven years old. My sister was in this play — *Our Town*. It made an impression on me. Are you awake?"

"Yes," she said, lying.

"I read the play because my sister was in it. She played a supporting part in it, not the lead, and I helped her practice her lines. So I learned her part and read the play. Are you listening?"

"Yes," she said, barely listening, "You helped her practice her lines."

"Right, I helped her practice her lines and by doing that I learned the play. It may have been the first play I ever read. Well, I didn't really read it, I helped her learn her lines and that's how I read it."

"That's how you read it," she repeated. Her eyes were almost closed now and his voice was becoming a distant memory.

"It changed my life, that play. Do you want to know why?" he asked, suddenly aware that he was speaking to himself, "Do you?"

"Yes," she said, startled, "it changed your life."

"It changed my life because of one scene. In this scene the lead character, a woman, Emily, dies, she dies in childbirth and the stage manager, he's kind of like God, he comes to her funeral along with all the people in her life. Are you listening?"

"Yes."

"He is at her funeral and — here's the weird part — *she's* also at her funeral. She's dead, but she still goes to her own funeral and she looks at all the people who are there — her mother, her friends and, most importantly, her husband. She sees her husband at her funeral. He's weeping. She died young and in childbirth, you see, so he's destroyed. And then, after a while, after she's been at her funeral a while, she asks the Stage Manager — this godlike character — if she can be alive again."

"What?"

"She wants to be alive again."

"Why?"

"Because she sees all the pain her death has caused and suddenly she misses life."

"Oh."

"So she asks God — the Stage Manager ... Do you understand what I'm saying?"

"Uh huh," she said, rousing herself, "Yes — she goes to a funeral."

"She goes to *her* funeral. She's dead!"

"She's dead? Oh yes — she's dead."

"And she asks the Stage Manager — the Stage Manager is like God or something like God — if she can live again."

"Yes — she wants to live again."

"Right. She's dead, but she wants to live again. And here is the great part. He agrees to let her live again, but she has to choose a day that is not important.

"What?"

"Not important. She can't choose her wedding day or the day she fell in love or lost her virginity or anything like that — she has to choose an ordinary day. A regular day. And guess what day she chooses?"

"What day?"

"Her thirteenth birthday."

"What?"

"Her thirteenth birthday."

"Why?"

"I don't know, they don't say, but she picks her thirteenth birthday as the day to go back and experience life. Of all the days of her life — she's dead, you remember — she picks her thirteenth birthday. Before marriage, before love, before puberty, before death — she picks her thirteenth birthday. The stage manager — God — agrees and lets her go back to that day. And here's the best part — she goes back to that day and realizes that during most of the day everyone ignores everyone else. No one realizes that life is slipping through their fingers. They don't understand how precious life is. Her brother who will die soon of appendicitis is still alive, but no one knows that he will die. Hell, he doesn't know he will die, and they all act as if they have all the time in the world — as if death will never happen — even though it will happen and has happened — and she knows it. And although she knows everything — that he will die and she will die — she has to relive the scene as she lived it. Are you listening?" he asked.

"What?" she said.

"Are you listening? Did you hear what I said? This is important."

"I'm listening," she said, exhausted.

"Yes, but did you hear about her going back."

"Yes, she had to live everything as before — right?" she asked, on the spot and feeling it.

"That's right," he said moving on, "she had to live it exactly as she had before although she knew that the way she had lived before was empty, a waste of time and not appreciative of life. She knew that they had wasted the time that they had together."

"I see," she said.

"And here's the best part," he said, "Finally, she asks God — the Stage Manager — to take her back."

"Back?" she asked.

"Back," he replied, "Back to her grave. She can't stand it anymore. She can't stand the pain of living her own life. She can't stand the pain of seeing how she wasted the precious moments that she had to enjoy life and cherish the people in her life. She can't stand it and asks the stage manager to take her back to her grave."

"She's upset."

"Yes, she's upset and she asks the Stage Manager, 'Do any human beings ever realize life while they live it? — every, every minute?'"

"Do they?" she asks, waking up slightly.

"'No,' he says. 'The saints and poets, maybe — they do some.' And then she says goodbye to life. She stands center stage and bids farewell to sunrises, sunsets, Grover's Corners — that's the name of "Our Town" — and summer and winter and rain and coffee. It breaks me up when she says goodbye to coffee."

"Why?" she said.

"Because it's so human," he said, "Coffee is so mundane, so ordinary — it's so perfect."

The girl didn't say anything. She was tired. She was tired because she had risen early, worked all day and his thoughts were exhausting. Still, she didn't say anything. She fought to keep her eyes open because she loved him and because he felt he was saying something important.

"It changed my life," he said; calm now, "it changed my life. Ever since I ran lines with my sister and saw that play, I've been different. I promised myself and that Stage Manager/God that I would live life to its fullest. I accepted the challenge. I would smell every rose, fight every fight and tell everyone that I loved, that I loved them. I swore I would appreciate every moment of life — every moment. That play, *Our Town*, changed my life."

"That's good, sweetheart," she said. "Can we go to bed now?"

"Yes," he said, "We can go to bed — now."

But he didn't go to bed. He petted his cats and he walked around their house. He stared into the darkness at the silhouettes that the plants made on the window shades. He didn't know what to do. She slept so easily. How could she sleep so easily? How could she waste the night with sleep?

Finally, he gravitated towards the bed. He sat on the edge of it and thought about what he should do. He could crawl into bed alongside the girl. He could stay awake all night. Yet, eventually he would sleep. Eventually life would demand that he give up and accept the obvious. As his head hit the pillow, he thought, "Live life while you can, enjoy life if you can, and make the most of life that you can."

Almost immediately, he fell fast asleep. And in his sleep, Emily and the Stage Manager visited him.

"Does he really think he can be the one who enjoys life to the fullest?" Emily asked.

"It's a dream," the Stage Manager said.

About the Author

Four-time Emmy®-award winning director and host Joseph Rosendo has been a travel, food and wine journalist and broadcaster since 1980. Since 2005, he has hosted,

directed and written *Joseph Rosendo's Travelscope®*, the award-winning travel television series. The series airs on PBS and Public Television stations in the U.S. and Canada, as well as in numerous international markets and streams worldwide on Amazon. The series continues to be one of the most entertaining, informative and thoughtful programs on television.

Since his first travel story appeared in *The Los Angeles Times*, Joseph has been published in countless publications and was the Consulting Editor for DK Eyewitness Travel Guides' *Where To Go When* and *Where To Go When — The Americas*, as well as the author of an *Insider's Guide to Los Angeles*.

For more than 23 years, as the creator and host of *Travelscope Radio*, he produced a weekly nationally syndicated travel show and features for numerous electronic media outlets including Discovery and the Associated Press. In addition, Joseph is the publisher of the *Travelscope Magazine*, a quarterly online travel, food and entertainment perspective, and contributes to *Travelscope.net* website where his blogs and podcasts are available.

Rosendo is a member of the prestigious Society of American Travel Writers and the Academy of Television Arts and Sciences. As a travel expert and motivational speaker, Joseph addresses national travel and wellness conferences, consumer shows and private gatherings. He lives in Topanga, California with his wife, Julie, and two spoiled ginger cats, Topanga Jones and Carlos. He welcomes questions and comments at: JRosendo@Travelscope.net.

 @Joseph Rosendo

 @Joseph Rosendo

 Travelscope

www.Travelscope.net

References

Achebach, J. (1993). Why Things Are, Volume II: The Big Picture. New York: Ballantine Books.

Albee, Edward (1958). *The Zoo Story*. New York: Samuel French.

Birnbaum, Steven (1980). *Get 'Em and Go Travel Guides*. Boston: Houghton Mifflin Co.

Borland, Hal (1965). *Countryman: A Summary of Belief*. Philadelphia: J. B. Lippincott Company.

Dickens, Charles (1843). *A Christmas Carol*. London: Chapman & Hall.

Emerson, Ralph Waldo. (1841; second series, 1844) *Essays, XII Art: page 435*. Boston: James Munroe.

Frost, Robert. (1915). *The Road Not Taken*. Boston: The Atlantic Monthly.

Herrick, Robert Herrick (1846). *Hesperides; or, the Works Both Human and Divine of Robert Herrick, Esq.* Publisher: William Pickering.

Heyward, DuBose and Dorothy. Gershwin, George and Ira. *Summertime* (from *Porgy and Bess*). Music and Lyrics by George Gershwin, DuBose and Dorothy Heyward and Ira Gershwin © 1938 (Renewed) Ira Gershwin Music, DuBose and Dorothy Heyward Memorial Fund and George Gershwin Music All Rights for Ira Gershwin Music Administered by WC Music Corp. All Rights Reserved Used by Permission of Alfred Music.

London, Jack (1905). *Getting Into Print*. New York: The Editor Publishing Company.

Lowell, James Russell (1857). *The Atlantic Monthly*. Boston: The Atlantic Monthly.

Massow, Rosalind (1985). *Travel Easy - The Practical Guide For People Over 50*. Washington, D.C.: American Association of Retired Persons.

McCarthy, Cormac (1994). *All the Pretty Horses*. New York: Vintage.

Muir, John (August 1897 issue). *The American Forest*. Washington D.C.: Atlantic Magazine.

Mozart, Wolfgang Amadé (1778). *The Letters of Mozart and His Family*. London: Macmillan and Company, limited, 1938.

Newman, Randy (1983). *I love L.A.* Hollywood: Warner Bros. Recording Studios.

Poe, Edgar Allan (1849). *Eldorado.* London: Hodder & Stoughton.

Priestly, J.B. (1929). *The Good Companions.* London: William Heinemann Ltd.

Seneca, Lucius Annaeus (c. AD 49). *De Brevitate Vitæ (On the shortness of life).* Francesco Baba, 1643.

Shakespeare, William (1623). *The Tragedy of Hamlet, Prince of Denmark.*

Signman, Carl and Magidson, Herb (1949). *Enjoy Yourself (It's Later Than You Think).*

Swift, Jonathan (1738). *The Colonel, in Polite Conversation, dialogue 2*

Thomas, Dylan (1937). *The Poems of Dylan Thomas.* New York: New Directions Publishing Corp.

Thompson, Hunter S. (1998) *The Proud Highway: Saga of a Desperate Southern Gentleman, 1955-1967 (The Fear and Loathing Letters #1).* New York: Penguin Random House.

Thoreau, Henry David (1854). *Walden; or, Life in the Woods,* series of 18 essays. Boston: Ticknor and Fields.

Twain, Mark (1869). *The Innocents Abroad, or The New Pilgrims' Progress.* Hartford, Connecticut: American Publishing Company.

Wilder, Thornton. Excerpts from *Our Town* by Thornton Wilder. Copyright © 1938 by The Wilder Family LLC Reprinted by arrangement with The Wilder Family LLC and The Barbara Hogenson Agency, Inc. All rights reserved.

Wilson, Harvey Earl (1961). *It Happened Last Night*. New York: syndicated columnist.

Wolfe, Thomas (1940). *You Can't Go Home Again*. New York: Harper & Row.

John 16:33 (KJV). *Deuteronomy 30:19* (KJV). *23rd Psalm* (KJV). Scripture quotations and references in this book were taken from the 21st Century King James Version®, copyright ©1994. Used by permission of Deuel Enterprises, Inc., Gary, SD 57237. All rights reserved.

1 Corinthians 13:13
Scriptural excerpts from *1 Corinthians* were taken from the American Standard Version published in 1901 by Thomas Nelson & Sons. Translations were found at https://www.biblegateway.com.

CPSIA information can be obtained
at www.ICGtesting.com
Printed in the USA
LVHW051929280122
709476LV00011B/1181